T0260469

Real-World Hadoop

Ted Dunning and Ellen Friedman

Beijing · Cambridge · Farnham · Köln · Sebastopol · Tokyo

Real-World Hadoop

by Ted Dunning and Ellen Friedman

Printed in the United States of America.

Published by O'Reilly Media, Inc., 1005 Gravenstein Highway North, Sebastopol, CA 95472.

O'Reilly books may be purchased for educational, business, or sales promotional use. Online editions are also available for most titles (*http://safaribooksonline.com*). For more information, contact our corporate/institutional sales department: 800-998-9938 or *corporate@oreilly.com*.

Editors: Mike Hendrickson and Tim Mc-Govern	**Interior Designer:** David Futato
Cover Designer: Karen Montgomery	**Illustrator:** Rebecca Demarest

January 2015:   First Edition

Revision History for the First Edition:

2015-01-26:   First release

2015-03-18:   Second release

See *http://oreilly.com/catalog/errata.csp?isbn=9781491922668* for release details.

ISBN: 978-1-491-92266-8

[LSI]

The authors dedicate this book with gratitude to Yorick Wilks, Fellow of the British Computing Society and Professor Emeritus in the Natural Language Processing Group at University of Sheffield, Senior Research Fellow at the Oxford Internet Institute, Senior Research Scientist at the Florida Institute for Human and Machine Cognition, and an extraordinary person.

Yorick mentored Ted Dunning as Department Chair and his graduate advisor during Ted's doctoral studies in Computing Science at the University of Sheffield. He also provided guidance as Ted's supervisor while Yorick was Director of the Computing Research Laboratory, New Mexico State University, where Ted did research on statistical methods for natural language processing (NLP). Yorick's strong leadership showed that critical and open examination of a wide range of ideas is the foundation of real progress. Ted can only hope to try to live up to that ideal.

We both are grateful to Yorick for his outstanding and continuing contributions to computing science, especially in the fields of artificial intelligence and NLP, through a career that spans five decades. His brilliance in research is matched by a sparkling wit, and it is both a pleasure and an inspiration to know him.

These links provide more details about Yorick's work:

http://staffwww.dcs.shef.ac.uk/people/Y.Wilks/

http://en.wikipedia.org/wiki/Yorick_Wilks

Table of Contents

Preface

This book is for you if you are interested in how Apache Hadoop and related technologies can address problems involving large-scale data in cost-effective ways. Whether you are new to Hadoop or a seasoned user, you should find the content in this book both accessible and helpful.

Here we speak to business team leaders, CIOs, business analysts, and technical developers to explain in basic terms how NoSQL Apache Hadoop and Apache HBase–related technologies work to meet big data challenges and the ways in which people are using them, including using Hadoop in production. Detailed knowledge of Hadoop is not a prerequisite for this book. We do assume you are rougly familiar with what Hadoop and HBase are, and we focus mainly on how best to use them to advantage. The book includes some suggestions for best practice, but it is intended neither as a technical reference nor a comprehensive guide to how to use these technologies, and people can easily read it whether or not they have a deeply technical background. That said, we think that technical adepts will also benefit, not so much from a review of tools, but from a sharing of experience.

Based on real-world situations and experience, in this book we aim to describe how Hadoop-based systems and new NoSQL database technologies such as Apache HBase have been used to solve a wide variety of business and research problems. These tools have grown to be very effective and production-ready. Hadoop and associated tools are being used successfully in a variety of use cases and sectors. To choose to move into these new approaches is a big decision, and the first step is to recognize how these solutions can be an advantage to achieve your own specific goals. For those just getting started, we describe some of the pre-planning and early decisions that can make the process easier and more productive. People who are already using Hadoop and NoSQL-based technologies will find suggestions for new ways to gain the full range of benefits possible from employing Hadoop well.

In order to help inform the choices people make as they consider these new solutions, we've put together:

- An overview of the reasons people are turning to these technologies
- A brief review of what the Hadoop ecosystem tools can do for you
- A collection of tips for success
- A description of some widely applicable prototypical use cases
- Stories from the real world to show how people are already using Hadoop and NoSQL successfully for experimentation, development, and in production

This book is a selection of various examples that should help guide decisions and spark your ideas for how best to employ these technologies. The examples we describe are based on how customers use the Hadoop distribution from MapR Technologies to solve their big data needs in many situations across a range of different sectors. The uses for Hadoop we describe are not, however, limited to MapR. Where a particular capability is MapR-specific, we call that to your attention and explain how this would be handled by other Hadoop distributions. Regardless of the Hadoop distribution you choose, you should be able to see yourself in these examples and gain insights into how to make the best use of Hadoop for your own purposes.

How to Use This Book

If you are inexperienced with Apache Hadoop and NoSQL nonrelational databases, you will find basic advice to get you started, as well as suggestions for planning your use of Hadoop going forward.

If you are a seasoned Hadoop user and have familiarity with Hadoop-based tools, you may want to mostly skim or even skip Chapter 2 except as a quick review of the ecosystem.

For all readers, when you reach Chapter 5 and Chapter 6, consider them together. The former explains some of the most rewarding of prototypical Hadoop use cases so that you see what your options are.

Chapter 6 then shows you how Hadoop users are putting those options together in real-world settings to address many different problems.

We hope you find this approach helpful.

—Ted Dunning and Ellen Friedman, January 2015

CHAPTER 1

Turning to Apache Hadoop and NoSQL Solutions

Some questions are easier to answer than others. In response to the question, *"Is Hadoop ready for production?,"* the answer is, simply, "yes."

This answer may surprise you, given how young the Apache Hadoop technology actually is. You may wonder on what basis we offer this definitive response to the question of Hadoop's readiness for production. The key reason we say that it is ready is simply because so many organizations are already using Hadoop in production and doing so successfully. Of course, being ready for production is not the same thing as being a mature technology.

Will Hadoop-based technologies change over the next few years? Of course they will. This is a rapidly expanding new arena, with continual improvements in the underlying technology and the appearance of innovative new tools that run in this ecosystem. The level of experience and understanding among Hadoop users is also rapidly increasing. As Hadoop and its related technologies continue progress toward maturity, there will be a high rate of change. Not only will new features and capabilities be added, these technologies will generally become easier to use as they become more refined.

Are these technologies a good choice for you? The answer to that question is more complicated, as it depends on your own project goals, your resources, and your willingness to adopt new approaches. Even with a mature technology, there would be a learning curve to account for in planning the use of something different; with a maturing technology you also have to account for a cost of novelty and stay adaptable to rapid change in the technology. Hadoop and NoSQL solutions are still young, so not only are the tools themselves still somewhat short of maturity, there is also a more limited pool of experienced users from which to select when building out your own team than with some older approaches.

Even so, Hadoop adoption is widespread and growing rapidly. For many, the question is no longer whether or not to turn to Hadoop and NoSQL solutions for their big data challenges but rather, *"What are the best ways to use Hadoop and NoSQL to carry our projects successfully?"* and *"When should we start?"*

This book aims to help answer these questions by providing a conversation around the choices that drive success in big data projects, by sharing tips that others have found useful, and by examining a selection of use cases and stories from successful Hadoop-based projects. What makes this collection of use cases different is that we include examples of how people are already using Hadoop in production and in near-production settings. We base our stories and recommendations on the experiences of real teams running real workloads. Of course, we do not focus only on Hadoop in production—we also provide advice to help you get started and to use Hadoop successfully in development.

When is the time right to give Hadoop a try? There is no "right" answer to that question, as each situation is different, but now may be a good time to give Hadoop a try even if you're not yet ready to consider it in a production setting for your own projects. If you start now, you will not be a Hadoop pioneer—the true pioneers are the ones already using it in production. But there is still an early-mover advantage to be had for those starting now. For one thing, you will find out if this technology holds promise for your situation. For another, you will begin building Hadoop expertise within your organization, which may prove very valuable. Even if you do not at present have an urgent need for a Hadoop-based solution, it's very likely you will need it or a solution similar to it soon. Having teams who are savvy about using Hadoop is an investment in the future.

A Day in the Life of a Big Data Project

Before we look in detail at what Hadoop is and how you might use it, let's start with a look at an unusual Hadoop-based project that is changing society in fundamental ways. The story begins with this challenge: suppose you need to be able to identify every person in India, uniquely and reliably—all 1.2 billion of them. And suppose you need to be able to authenticate this identification for any individual who requests it, at any time, from any place in India, in less than a second. Does this sound sufficiently challenging?

That description is the central mission for India's Aadhaar project, the Unique Identification Authority of India (UIDAI). The project provides a unique 12-digit, government-issued identification number that is tied to biometric data to verify the identity and address for each person in India. The biometric data includes an iris scan of both eyes plus multipoint data from the fingerprint pattern of all 10 fingers, as suggested by the illustration in Figure 1-1. The unique Aadhaar ID number is a random number, and it is assigned without classification based on caste, religion, or creed, assuring an openness and equality to the project.

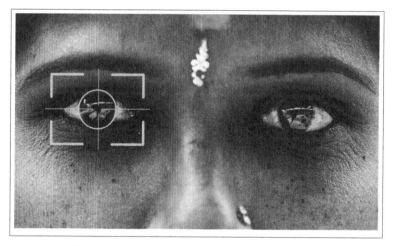

Figure 1-1. Unique Identification Authority of India (UIDAI) is running the Aadhaar project, whose goal is to provide a unique 12-digit identification number plus biometric data to authenticate to every one of the roughly 1.2 billion people in India. This is the largest scale ever reached by a biometric system. (Figure based on image by Christian Als/Panos Pictures.)

The need for such an identification program and its potential impact on society is enormous. In India, there is no social security card, and much of the population lacks a passport. Literacy rates are relatively low, and the population is scattered across hundreds of thousands of villages. Without adequately verifiable identification, it has been difficult for many citizens to set up a bank account or otherwise participate in a modern economy.

For India's poorer citizens, this problem has even more dire consequences. The government has extensive programs to provide widespread relief for the poor—for example, through grain subsidies to those who are underfed and through government-sponsored work programs for the unemployed. Yet many who need help do not have access to benefit programs, in part because of the inability to verify who they are and whether they qualify for the programs. In addition, there is a huge level of so-called "leakage" of government aid that disappears to apparent fraud. For example, it has been estimated that over 50% of funds intended to provide grain to the poor goes missing, and that fraudulent claims for "ghost workers" siphon off much of the aid intended to create work for the poor.

The Aadhaar program is poised to change this. It is in the process of creating the largest biometric database in the world, one that can be leveraged to authenticate identities for each citizen, even on site in rural villages. A wide range of mobile devices from cell phones to micro scanners can be used to enroll people and to authenticate their identities when a transaction is requested. People will be able to make payments at remote sites via micro-ATMs. Aadhaar ID authentication will be used to verify qualification for relief food deliveries and to provide pension payments for the elderly. Implementation of this massive digital identification system is expected to save the equivalent of millions and perhaps billions of dollars each year by thwarting efforts at fraud. While the UIDAI project will have broad benefits for the Indian society as a whole, the greatest impact will be for the poorest people.

The UIDAI project is a Hadoop-based program that is well into production. At the time of this writing, over 700 million people have been enrolled and their identity information has been verified. The target is to reach a total of at least 100 crore (1 billion) enrollments during 2015. Currently the enrollment rate is about 10 million people every 10 days, so the project is well positioned to meet that target.

From a technical point of view, what are the requirements for such an impressive big data project? Scalability and reliability are among the most significant requirements, along with capability for very high performance. This challenge starts with the enrollment process itself. Once address and biometric data are collected for a particular individual, the enrollment must undergo deduplication. Deduplication for each new enrollment requires the processing of comparisons against billions of records. As the system grows, deduplication becomes an even greater challenge.

Meanwhile, the Aadhaar digital platform is also busy handling authentication for each transaction conducted by the millions of people already enrolled. Authentication involves a profile lookup, and it is required to support thousands of concurrent transactions with response times on the order of 100ms. The authentication system was designed to run on Hadoop and Apache HBase. It currently uses the MapR distribution for Hadoop. Rather than employ HBase, the authentication system uses MapR-DB, a NoSQL database that supports the HBase API and is part of MapR. We'll delve more into how MapR-DB and other technologies interrelate later in this chapter and in Chapter 2. In addition to being able to handle the authentication workload, the Aadhaar authentication system also has to meet strict availability requirements, provide robustness in the face of machine failure, and operate across multiple datacenters.

Chief Architect of the Aadhaar project, Pramod Varma, has pointed out that the project is "built on sound strategy and a strong technology backbone." The most essential characteristics of the technology involved in Aadhaar are to be highly available and to be able to deliver sub-second performance.

From Aadhaar to Your Own Big Data Project

The Aadhaar project is not only an impressive example of vision and planning, it also highlights the ability of Hadoop and NoSQL solutions to meet the goals of an ambitious program. As unusual as this project seems—not everyone is trying to set up an identification program for a country the size of India—there are commonalities between this unusual project and more ordinary projects both in terms of the nature of the problems being addressed and the design of successful solutions. In other words, in this use case, as in the others we discuss, you should be able to see your own challenges even if you work in a very different sector.

One commonality is data size. As it turns out, while Aadhaar is a large-scale project with huge social impact and fairly extreme requirements for high availability and performance, as far as data volume goes, it is not unusually large among big data projects. Data volumes in the financial sector, for instance, are often this size or even larger because so many transactions are involved. Similarly, machine-produced data in the area of the industrial Internet can easily exceed the volumes of Aadhaar. The need for reliable scalability in India's project applies to projects in these cases as well.

Other comparisons besides data volume can be drawn between Aadhaar and more conventional use cases. If you are involved with a large retail business, for instance, the idea of identity or profile lookup is quite familiar. You may be trying to optimize an advertising campaign, and as part of the project you need to look up the profiles of customers to verify their location, tastes, or buying behaviors, possibly at even higher rates than needed by Aadhaar. Such projects often involve more than simple verification, possibly relying on complex analytics or machine learning such as predictive filtering, but the need to get the individual profile data for a large number of customers is still an essential part of implementing such a solution. The challenging performance requirements of Aadhaar are also found in a wide range of projects. In these situations, a Hadoop-based NoSQL solution such as HBase or MapR-DB provides the ability to scale horizontally to meet the needs of large volume data and to avoid traffic problems that can reduce performance.

What Hadoop and NoSQL Do

The most fundamental reason to turn to Hadoop is for the ability to handle very large-scale data at reasonable cost in a reasonable time. The same applies to Hadoop-based NoSQL database management solutions such as HBase and MapR-DB. There are other choices for large-scale distributed computing, including Cassandra, Riak, and more, but Hadoop-based systems are widely used and are the focus of our book. Figure 1-2 shows how interest in Hadoop has grown, based on search terms used in Google Trends.

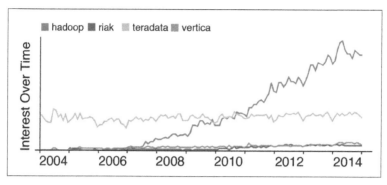

Figure 1-2. Google Trends shows a sharp rise in popularity of the term "hadoop" in searches through recent years, suggesting an increased interest in Hadoop as a technology. We did not include "cassandra" as a search term because its popularity as a personal name means there is no easy way to disambiguate results for the database from results for human names.

In addition to the ability to store large amounts of data in a cost-effective way, Hadoop also provides mechanisms to greatly improve computation performance at scale. Hadoop involves a distributed storage layer plus a framework to coordinate that storage. In addition, Hadoop provides a computational framework to support parallel processing. In its original form, Hadoop was developed as an open source Apache Foundation project based on Google's MapReduce paradigm. Today there are a variety of different distributions for Hadoop.

One of the key aspects of this distributed approach to computation involves dividing large jobs into a collection of smaller tasks that can be run in parallel, completely independently of each other. The outputs of these tasks are shuffled and then processed by other tasks. By running tasks in parallel, jobs can be completed more quickly, which allows the system to have very high throughput. The original Hadoop MapReduce provided a framework that allowed programs to be built in a relatively straightforward way that could run in this style and thus provided highly scalable computation. MapReduce programs run in batch, and they are useful for aggregation and counting at large scale.

Another key factor for performance is the ability to move the computation to where the data is stored rather than having to move data to the computation. In traditional computing systems, data storage is segregated from computational systems. With Hadoop, there is no such segregation, and programs can run on the same machines that store the data. The result is that you move only megabytes of program instead of terabytes of data in order to do a very large-scale computation, which results in greatly improved performance.

The original Hadoop MapReduce implementation was innovative but also fairly limited and inflexible. MapReduce provided a start and was good enough to set in motion a revolution in scalable computing. With recent additions to the Hadoop ecosystem, more advanced and more flexible systems are also becoming available. MapReduce is, however, still an important method for aggregation and counting, particularly in certain situations where the batch nature of MapReduce is not a problem. More importantly, the basic ideas on which MapReduce is based—parallel processing, data locality, and the shuffle and reassembly of results—can also be seen underlying new computational tools such as Apache Spark, Apache Tez, and Apache Drill. Most likely, more tools that take advantage of these basic innovations will also be coming along.

All of these computational frameworks run on the Hadoop storage layer, as shown in Figure 1-3. An important difference in these new systems is that they avoid storing every intermediate result to disk, which in turn provides improved speed for computation. Another difference is that the new systems allow computations to be chained more flexibly. The effect of these differences is better overall performance in some situations and applicability to a wider range of problems.

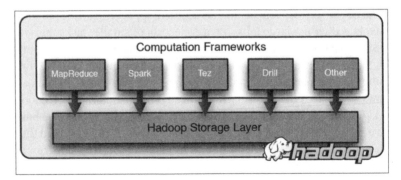

Figure 1-3. A variety of different computational frameworks for parallel processing are available to run on the Apache Hadoop storage layer for large data systems.

In addition to the ability to scale horizontally at low cost and to perform large-scale computations very efficiently and rapidly, Hadoop-based technologies are also changing the game by encouraging the use of new types of data formats. Both files and NoSQL databases allow you to use a wide range of data formats, including unstructured or semistructured data. Concurrent with the development of Hadoop's computational capabilities, there have been dramatic improvements in our understanding of how to store data in flat files and NoSQL databases. These new ways for structuring data greatly expand the options and provide a greater degree of flexibility than you may be used to. We say more about new data formats among the tips in Chapter 4.

NoSQL nonrelational databases can augment the capabilities of the flat files with the ability to access and update a subset of records, each identified by a unique key, rather than having to scan an entire file as you would with flat files.

With their ability to scale in a cost-effective way and to handle unstructured data, NoSQL databases provide a powerful solution for a variety of use cases, but they should not be thought of as a replacement for the function of traditional databases. This distinction is described in more detail in Chapter 2, but the essential point to note is that each of these technologies—NoSQL databases and traditional relational databases (RDBMS)—should be used for the things they do best. Some NoSQL databases have a better ability to scale and to do so while keeping costs down. They can handle raw, unstructured data that also affects use cases for which they are well suited. In contrast, there is a price to be paid with RDBMS (literally and in terms of the effort required for processing and structuring data for loading). The reward for this cost, however, can be extremely good performance with RDBMS for specific, highly defined tasks such as critical path billing and standardized reporting. However, to get these benefits, the data must already be prepared for the tasks.

When Are Hadoop and NoSQL the Right Choice?

The need to handle large amounts of data cost effectively has led to the development of scalable distributed computing systems such as those discussed in this book, based on Hadoop and on NoSQL databases. But these new technologies are proving so effective that they go beyond providing solutions for existing projects; they are inviting exploration into new problems that previously would have seemed impractical to consider.

A key distinction of these systems from previous ones is flexibility. This flexibility is manifested in the platform itself through the capability to handle new data types and multiple computational models, as well as to scale to very large data sizes. Hadoop adds flexibility in your choices by being able to store essentially "raw" data and make decisions about how to process and use it later. Flexibility is also manifested in the ways that developers are combining diverse data streams and new analysis techniques in a single platform. In the MapR distribution for Hadoop, there is further flexibility to use existing non-Hadoop applications side by side on the same systems and operate on the same data as Hadoop applications.

Chapter 2 provides you with an overview of the functions supported by Hadoop ecosystem tools, while Chapter 3 explains some of the extra capabilities of MapR's distribution so that you will be better able to extrapolate from our examples to your own situation, whichever Hadoop distribution you choose to try. In Chapter 4, we provide a list of tips for success when working with Hadoop that offer help for newcomers and for experienced Hadoop users.

In order to help you better understand how these technologies may bring value to your own projects, this book also describes a selection of Hadoop use cases based on how MapR customers are using it. MapR currently has over 700 paying customers across a wide range of sectors including financial services, web-based businesses, manufacturing, media, telecommunications, and retail. Based on those, we have identified a variety of key usage patterns that we describe in Chapter 5 as well as telling example stories in Chapter 6 that show how customers combine these solutions to meet their own big data challenges.

Are the examples described in this book MapR specific? For the most part, no. There are some aspects of what people are doing that rely on specific MapR features or behaviors, but we've tried to call those to your attention and point out what the alternatives would be. The use cases and customer stories have been chosen to show the power of Hadoop and NoSQL solutions to provide new ways to solve problems at scale. Regardless of the Hadoop distribution you choose, the material in this book should help guide you in the decisions you'll need to make in order to plan well and execute successful big data projects.

CHAPTER 2

What the Hadoop Ecosystem Offers

Apache Hadoop and related technologies are rapidly evolving, and as such they are spawning a large array of new tools. As people see growing value and expanding use cases in this area, the number of tools to address significant needs also grows. This trend is good news in that it provides a wide range of functions to support the activities you may want to carry out in this new arena. However, the wealth of new and unfamiliar tools can feel a bit overwhelming.

In order to help guide you through the choices being offered in the Hadoop ecosystem in a meaningful way, we take a look here at some of the key actions that are commonly desired in Hadoop and NoSQL use cases and provide you with a description of some of the tools widely used to carry out those operations. This is by no means a full catalog of what's available, nor is it a how-to manual for using the tools. Instead, our focus is on the issues associated with functions common to many Hadoop-based projects. This high-level view of what various Hadoop ecosystem tools are used for is intended to help you to assess tools of interest to you, whether or not they're included in our list, in terms of how they may be helpful for your projects.

To get started, we've put together a chart of some major needs that are common to many use cases and that shows you a few of the tools associated with each one. In Table 2-1, a selection of the most prominent tools in the Hadoop ecosystem are broken down roughly by time-scale and by their typical purposes.

Table 2-1. Hadoop ecosystem tools broken down by time-scale and general purpose. Note that all tools generally work on all platforms, with a few exceptions. For instance, NFS and direct file access allow realtime updates and POSIX semantics on MapR but not on other platforms. Also, some interface methods such as ODBC and NFS (depending on platform, as noted) open up a huge range of tools. Note that Impala and ElasticSearch are open source with a closed community. MapR-DB, Teradata, and Tableau are closed source. The rest listed here are fully open source projects.

	Ingest	Process	Persist	Extract
Batch	Flume, sqoop, Kafka, NFS	Hive, Pig	Files	NFS, Teradata, and other connectors
Ad hoc	Flume, NFS	Spark, Impala, Drill, Hive (soon), Solr, ElasticSearch	File, HBase, MapR-DB	ODBC tools such as Tableau, direct web access
Streaming and realtime	Flume, Kafka, NFS	Spark streaming, Storm, Samza	HBase, MapR-DB, file (on some platforms)	HBase, MapR-DB, NFS

Typical Functions

Table 2-1 divides the functions to be done in big data applications into *ingestion*, *data processing or transformation*, *persistence*, and *extraction*. Ingestion is the process of getting data into a system with minimal processing or transformation applied during ingestion. Processing is where all significant computing and transformation is done. The most common operation in processing raw data is that it is aggregated into summaries or arranged into profiles. Data is commonly persisted after processing, but in Hadoop systems, data is also commonly persisted in nearly raw form as it is ingested but before it is processed. The retention of relatively raw data makes it possible for errors in stream processing to be corrected. It is also advantageous in that it widens the opportunities for data exploration and avoids discarding data that may later be of great value, as we discuss further in Chapter 4, Chapter 5, and Chapter 6.

Different forms of persistence lend themselves to different kinds of processing. For example, files can be used to achieve very high scan rates that are particularly useful in batch programming, while HBase or MapR-DB are very useful in real time or streaming processing where updates may have to be made each time a record is processed.

Finally, data must somehow be transmitted to other systems via some form of extraction.

For each kind of function, it is typical that the tool of choice depends strongly on the time scale in which the processing must be done.

The time scale dealt with in Table 2-1 ranges from batch, through ad hoc, to streaming and realtime. Batch processing is typically done on all the data that accumulates over a period of minutes to days or even a month or longer. The emphasis in batch processing is total throughput, and it usually doesn't matter how long it takes to process any single input record as long many records are processed quickly.

In ad hoc processing, the emphasis is on a quick (in human terms) response, but the data being processed is very much like the input for a batch process in that it typically consists of all of the data available or all of the data for a recent time period. In fact, ad hoc processing can be thought of as batch processing that is initiated by some user action instead of being based on a schedule. Ad hoc processing is sometimes mislabeled as realtime because there is a user-visible response time, but this is a serious misnomer that could lead to some confusion about which tool is appropriate to use.

With streaming or realtime processing, records are processed as they arrive or in very small batches known as micro batches. Realtime processing adds the additional constraint that records must not only be processed as they arrive, but that processing must complete before a pre-specified deadline passes. Requiring that records be processed one at a time is more expensive than processing large batches of records since it does not allow certain economies of scale that are possible in batch processing.

The rest of this chapter will provide a quick inventory of the tools used in the Hadoop ecosystem to carry out these functions.

Data Storage and Persistence

The most obvious requirement for data storage in this new arena is for scalability, both in terms of starting with large amounts of data and in being able to adapt to growing data volumes in future. For large-scale and long-term storage, reliability is, of course, a critical requirement for most projects.

Data storage comes in different forms that have different virtues. Storage as files has the virtue of being fast to scan and is therefore well suited for batch processing. It is difficult, however, to find a particular record in large input files or to find a number of records that pertain to a single individual. Furthermore, updates to files can be difficult to coordinate. These actions are much better supported by some sort of database, and in the Hadoop ecosystem, that means Apache HBase or MapR-DB. Reading or updating single records is easy with these NoSQL databases at the significant cost in scanning performance relative to flat files.

Another aspect of storage that is almost as important as scalability is the shift toward storing a wide variety of data sources, including unstructured or semistructured data. This change in what is being stored also reflects the change in when data is processed: in these systems, the storage layer is often used to store raw data at scale and persist it for long periods of time in a relatively raw form. Choices about how to process, extract, and analyze data come after this "ingestion" step, which is a very different approach than the extract, transform, and load (ETL) process that is usual for traditional relational databases, for instance. The traditional style of ETL processing is not required for storage in Hadoop-based systems, although using Hadoop to do ETL *for a traditional RDBMS resource* is a widely beneficial Hadoop use case (more on that in Chapter 5).

For highly scalable flat file storage, the tools of interest here are Hadoop-based. These are Hadoop Distributed File System (HDFS) or the storage layer of the MapR distribution of Hadoop (MapR-FS). Files in both of these systems can be created and accessed using the HDFS API or, in the case of MapR-FS, files also can be created, accessed, and updated using standard file operations via the network file system (NFS).

For persistence of data in a nonrelational NoSQL database, there are a number of popular non-Hadoop choices, including Cassandra, Riak, or the Hadoop-based NoSQL databases such as HBase or MapR-DB, a NoSQL database integrated into the MapR file system.

As mentioned briefly in Chapter 1, NoSQL databases are not intended to completely replace relational databases. Each has its own strengths and should be used for what it does best. NoSQL databases generally have given up some of the capabilities of relational databases such as advanced indexing and transactions in order to allow them to scale to much higher throughput and data sizes than are possible with relational systems.

The data stored in files or NoSQL databases is often very different from the data stored in a traditional relational database. Somewhat ironically, the term "structured" data is typically used to refer to data in traditional records with fields containing primitive values. Data with substantial free-form components such as text is often called "unstructured." The term "semistructured" refers to data that has records with fields but where different records may have different collections of fields, and the contents of the fields may contain sub-fields or lists of record-like objects.

Semistructured data is more expressive than structured data, but it cannot easily be manipulated by traditional query languages like SQL. The expressivity of semistructured data can be a particular advantage in big data systems because it allows data to be denormalized. Denormalization can involve the inclusion of redundant data. For example, more data may be stored inline, which in turn decreases the degree to which other data sources must be referenced in order to understand the data. The advantages of denormalization can include improved read performance, plus it can allow storing data in its natural state, thus preserving potentially useful information. This is particularly important with flat files and with NoSQL databases, not only because it makes data easier to understand, but also precisely because flat files and NoSQL databases typically lack the strong ability of *relational* databases for records to have references to other records.

> To succeed in big data, it is very important to come to understand both the advantages and the problems of semistructured data.

The use cases in this book will highlight many of the ways that semistructured data can be used for big-data applications.

Data Ingest

Storing data is useful, but unless the data is manufactured from nothing, you have to get it into your cluster from somewhere else. Exactly how you get it in depends on where the data is coming from and how you need to use it.

As shown in Table 2-1, the best choice of ingest method depends in part on whether you are dealing with batch, ad hoc, or streaming and realtime processes. There are several tools that have been developed specifically for ingesting data into Hadoop, but these Hadoop-specific tools were built with the assumption of batch programming that can limit their utility if you need realtime ingestion. In addition to specialized tools for data ingestion, some Hadoop distributions offer NFS access to the cluster. This can be a good way to get realtime ingestion using standard file-oriented Linux tools, but only if the underlying distributed file system is a realtime file system. For the Hadoop-in-production stories discussed in this book, we've drawn from the experience of companies who use the MapR distribution for Hadoop and are therefore using a realtime distributed file system in the form of MapR-FS.

A function that is needed in the case of streaming data ingestion (or export from a realtime analytics application) is to provide a queuing layer. The benefits of queuing are described in more detail in the tips presented in Chapter 4. Two of the tools listed here, Apache Kafka and Apache Flume, are useful to provide a queue.

Some of the widely used tools for data ingestion in Hadoop are described in detail in the sections that follow.

Apache Kafka

Kafka is a robust pub-sub (publish, subscribe) framework that allows highly available, dependable message streaming. It is a paradox that a key feature of Kakfa is its small number of features. It has far fewer features and is much less configurable than Flume, which is described later. All Kafka does is store messages relatively reliably and at high volumes and rates. All computational considerations are outside of Kafka's scope. Such computation can be implemented using a variety of computational frameworks such as Spark Streaming, Apache Storm, or Apache Samza. This simplicity and focus of Kafka have helped make it very good at what it does.

There are a variety of programs in the Kafka ecosystem that support copying messages to a Hadoop cluster, but this is also commonly done as a side effect of processing messages.

Apache Sqoop

Sqoop is a batch-oriented program to import data from a database or export data back to a database. Sqoop can create files in a variety of formats in a Hadoop cluster. Sqoop is a very useful tool due to the wide range of databases that it supports, but Sqoop is, by design, entirely batch-oriented.

An interesting alternative to using Sqoop is to use database-specific export commands to export tables directly to a cluster or import them from the cluster using NFS. A virtue of this alternative approach is that it can be very high performance since databases generally have highly optimized table export/bulk import utilities. Using database export/import utilities will not, however, provide you with the native ability to store the resulting data in an advanced format such as Parquet.

Apache Flume

Flume is a complex tool that allows processing units to be strung together to transport data, typically with the aim of doing minimal ETL on the fly and then storing in HDFS files. Flume is nominally stream based, but a de facto batch orientation is often imposed by storing data in HDFS files. If data is pushed instead into a pub-sub framework like Kafka, then true streaming operation can be achieved. Flume has limited and complex provisions for high availability and guaranteed delivery. Flume was originally limited to processing textual data arranged one record per line as is normally done in log files, and there are still echoes of this limitation in various parts of the framework. In general, the complexity of Flume makes the use of Kafka plus either Storm or Spark Streaming a preferable option.

Data Extraction from Hadoop

Data can be extracted from a Hadoop cluster using Sqoop to move data into a database. NFS access is another good way to get data out of a Hadoop cluster if you are using MapR. To export file data on other systems, you can use the command line tools that come with Hadoop distributions to copy individual files or directories of files.

Since the data being extracted from a cluster is typically much smaller than the data ingested into a cluster, the actual moving of the data out of the cluster is not usually a major concern. Getting the data into a file format that is accepted by other systems is typically a more important concern, but format conversion is relatively easy using systems like Apache Pig, Apache Drill, or Apache Hive.

Processing, Transforming, Querying

Processing of data in a Hadoop cluster can be done in a variety of ways including streaming, micro-batched, batch mode, and by issuing interactive queries. The boundaries between these ways of processing data are not always completely sharp, but the basic distinctions are important to keep in mind. We mention a variety of tools to support each of these functions, and we call out several of the SQL-on-Hadoop query engines (Apache Drill, Apache Spark, and Impala) in more detail at the end of this section.

Streaming

In streaming processing, data is processed one record at a time. This is appropriate for simple enrichment, parsing or extraction, and simple aggregation, but many kinds of processing are not suitable for this style. It can also be difficult to make true streaming programs both efficient and restartable without losing data. Streaming processing of data does give the lowest latencies, however, so when latencies really need to be less than a second or so, streaming may be the best option. Currently Apache Storm is the de facto standard for true streaming processing, while Spark Streaming is probably the most common micro-batching environment, as described next.

Micro-batching

Micro-batching involves processing all the records from a short time period (typically seconds to minutes) in a batch. Micro-batching usually has real problems providing very low latency, but it does provide a much simpler environment than streaming, especially when high availability is required. If your use case allows for tens of seconds of latency, then micro-batching with a tool such as Spark Streaming can be ideal.

Batch Processing

True batch processing is typically used for computing complex aggregates or when training models. Batch processing is typically initiated every hour, day, week, or month and computes summaries of large amounts of data accumulated over long time periods. Batch processing is often combined with stream processing or micro-batching in what is known as the lambda architecture to allow small errors in the streaming computation to be corrected. These errors are often due to delays in receiving incoming data or failover or upgrade of some component of the cluster supporting the streaming computation. By allowing small errors to be corrected by a batch process, the system doing the streaming processing can often be made much simpler. Batch processing is most commonly implemented using Apache Hive, Apache Spark, or Apache Pig.

Interactive Query

In some cases, users require the ability to perform bespoke aggregation operations on data according to whatever analysis they are working on at the moment. In such cases, neither batch nor streaming models are particularly appropriate. Instead, an interactive compute model is required with quick response. This is a change from streaming and micro-batching models that makes results available shortly after the data arrives, but where the programs are provided long in advance. Instead, interactive computing provides results shortly after the query arrives and assumes that the data is already in place. Interactive queries are commonly custom aggregations and are often generated by visualization tools. The most common systems for interactive querying are Impala, Apache Spark, and Apache Drill.

Impala

Impala is a system that is designed to scan flat files at a very high rate to compute the result of aggregation queries written in SQL. The preferred format for data to be queried by Impala is Parquet, and Impala is able to use the features of Parquet to great advantage to accelerate the scanning of large files. For the most part, Impala uses the table management capabilities of Hive to define tables and their schema. The data model used by Impala is currently very similar to the model used by relational systems, but extension beyond the relational model, including nested data, is planned.

Apache Drill

Apache Drill is a newly graduated top-level Apache project that offers the user an unusual level of flexibility. It provides standard SQL (not SQL-like) query capabilities that can access a surprisingly diverse range of data sources and formats, including nested formats such as Parquet and JSON. Furthermore, Drill queries can be schema-less, allowing flexibility in data exploration. The Drill optimizer is a sophisticated cost-based optimizer that can radically restructure queries based on characteristics of the input files, and it is being extended to understand more about distributed query computation as the software grows further into maturity. Drill also offers useful extensibility, so it is a useful tool for business analysts as well as for developers. Like Impala, a key focus with Drill is to make the minimum response time very short so that it can be used for interactive purposes.

Apache Spark

Spark is an ambitious project that has defined an entire new computational framework for running programs in parallel. The key technical innovation in Spark is that it allows parallel datasets to be check-pointed implicitly by remembering how they were computed. In most cases, this avoids the need to write intermediate datasets to persistent storage such as disks, thus avoiding one of the traditional bottlenecks of Hadoop's MapReduce execution model. On top of the basic machinery of distributed in-memory datasets (known as RDDs for resilient distributed datasets) and a fast distributed execution engine, Spark has a large number of subprojects. One key subproject is SparkStreaming. SparkStreaming extends the concept of RDDs by defining D-streams as a sequence of RDDs. Each RDD in a D-stream can be acted on by a parallel program that allows computation to proceed as a series of very quick batch programs, or micro-batches.

Together this collection of query tools provides some attractive options. Impala and Drill allow SQL queries, while Spark allows queries to be written in the Scala programming language or in SQL. Spark and Drill can also be tightly integrated to get the best of both. Spark queries can be executed in micro-batched or interactive fashion. Together, these tools provide some very interesting possibilities.

Search Abuse—Using Search and Indexing for Interactive Query

Search engines are not normally considered as processing elements, but they can actually be used very nicely for many forms of interactive queries. Especially recently, both Apache Solr and ElasticSearch have added a variety of aggregation capabilities that can allow either system to be used to do simple aggregation queries.

These queries can be reported in the form of a graphical interface such as that provided by Kibana to produce very nice dashboard systems. These systems can also provide limited kinds of drill-down visualizations that can be very handy in situations where you are trying to zero in on the cause of some sort of anomaly.

Visualization Tools

One tool that blurs the batch/interactive boundary a bit is Datameer. Datameer provides an interactive approximation of large-scale computations combined with a suite of visualization tools. Designed for analysts who are most comfortable with advanced GUI tooling rather than programming, the Datameer system allows analysts who would otherwise be uncomfortable to build and run jobs either in batch mode or interactively.

Tableau is a widely used visualization product suite that provides interactive visualization tools that have previously been targeted at the analysis of data in data warehouses. With the emergence of interactive SQL query tools like Impala and Apache Drill that are accessible via ODBC, Tableau's tools can now analyze and visualize data on Hadoop clusters as well.

Integration via ODBC and JDBC

Apache Drill and Impala provide access to data on Hadoop clusters via the standard database access protocols ODBC or JDBC. Hive also provides limited access using these interfaces as well. ODBC was originally developed by Microsoft in the early '90s, but it is now widely used on other platforms as well. JDBC was created by Sun in the late '90s to provide a Java equivalent to ODBC. These protocols allow a wide range of standard tools that generate SQL queries to work with Hadoop. These include Tableau (mentioned above), Excel, Sqirrl, Toad, and many others. There are some speed bumps to keep in mind, however. By the nature of these interfaces, they cannot move very large amounts of data out of the cluster, but instead are more suited to invoking large-scale aggregations that return relatively small summaries of larger datasets. This limitation applies to any tool using ODBC or JDBC, of course, but the issue becomes more apparent when you are querying very large datasets, as is common with Hadoop clusters.

Accessing Hive (in particular via ODBC or JDBC) can be very frustrating since the number of simultaneous queries is severely limited by the way that queries are funneled through the HiveServer. Impala and Drill are much less subject to these limitations than Hive.

In general, the advantages of using ODBC and JDBC to connect a wide range of tools are substantial enough that these issues are likely to be addressed by vendors and the open source community before long.

CHAPTER 3

Understanding the MapR Distribution for Apache Hadoop

The Hadoop distribution provided by MapR Technologies contains Apache Hadoop and more. We're not just talking about the Hadoop ecosystem tools that ship with MapR—there are many, including almost all of those described in Chapter 2—but rather some special capabilities of MapR itself. These MapR-specific characteristics are the topic of this chapter because the real-world stories in this book are based on how MapR customers are using Apache Hadoop and the MapR NoSQL database, MapR-DB, to meet their large-scale computing needs in a variety of projects. The goal is to show you the benefits of Hadoop when used for the right jobs.

To make sure that you get the most out of this book, regardless of what kind of Hadoop distribution you use, we alert you to any aspects of the use cases we describe here that are not directly generalizable because of extra features of MapR not included in other distributions. For example, MapR is API-compatible with Hadoop, so applications written to run on Hadoop will run on MapR, but, in addition, non-Hadoop applications will also run on MapR, and that's unusual. We will describe how you might work around these issues if you are not using MapR.

Use of Existing Non-Hadoop Applications

One of the key distinctions with MapR is that it has a realtime, fully read-write filesystem. This means that you not only can interact with data stored on the cluster via Hadoop commands and applications, but you also can access data via traditional routes. Any program in any language that can access files on a Linux or Windows system can also access files in the MapR cluster using the same traditional mechanisms. This compatibility is made possible primarily because the MapR file system (MapR-FS) allows access to files via NFS. This is very different from HDFS, the file system that other major Hadoop distributions use for distributed data storage.

What are the implications of MapR-FS being a read/write POSIX file system accessible via NFS or Hadoop commands? One effect is that existing applications can be used directly, without needing to rewrite them as Hadoop applications. In contrast, when using with other Hadoop distributions, the workflow generally includes steps in which data is copied out of the Hadoop file system to local files to be available for traditional tools and applications. The output of these applications is then copied back into the HDFS cluster. This doesn't mean the use cases described in this book are only for MapR, but some of the details of the workflow may be somewhat different with other Hadoop distributions. For instance the workflow would need to include time to write Hadoop-specific code to access data and run applications, and the team doing so would need to be well versed in how HDFS file APIs differ from more traditional file APIs.

In case you are curious about the reason for this difference in MapR's ability to use traditional code, as well as some of MapR's other specific capabilities, here's a brief technical explanation. One key difference lies in the size of the units used to manipulate and track files in a MapR cluster as compared with HDFS. As illustrated in Figure 3-1, files in HDFS files are broken into blocks of a fixed size. The default value for these blocks is 128 megabytes. The value can be changed, but it still applies across all files in the cluster. The block size is fundamental to how HDFS tracks files in a central system called the name node. Every change in the size or other properties of the file aside from the content of the file itself must be sent to the name node in order to keep track of all pieces of all the files in the cluster. HDFS blocks are the unit of allocation, and once written, they are never updated. This has several logical consequences, including:

1. Realtime use of HDFS is difficult or impossible. This happens because every write to a file extends the length of the file when the write is committed. That means every such change requires talking to the name node, so programs try to avoid committing writes

too often. In fact, it is common for multiple blocks to be flushed at once.

2. The consistency model of HDFS is such that readers cannot be allowed to read files while a writer still has them open for writing.

3. Out-of-order writes cannot be allowed because they would constitute updates to the file.

4. A name node has to keep track of all of the blocks of all of the files, and because this information can churn rapidly while programs are running, this information has to be kept in memory. This means the name node's memory size is proportional to the number of blocks that can be tracked. That number times the block size is the scalability limit of an HDFS file system.

These consequences made HDFS much easier to implement originally, but they make it much harder for it to work in real time (which implies readers can see data instantly and writers can flush often), to scale to very large sizes (because of the limited number of blocks), or to support first-class access via NFS (because NFS inherently reorders writes and has no concept of an open file).

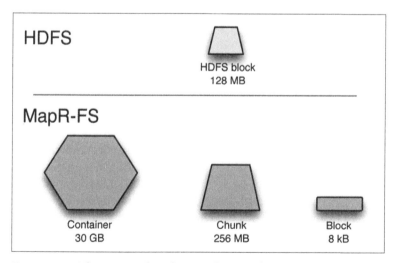

Figure 3-1. The MapR distribution for Apache Hadoop has a fully read/write realtime file system (MapR-FS). The MapR file system uses units of multiple sizes to organize its contents ranging from small (blocks of 8 kB) to very large (containers of 30 GB). Intermediate-

sized units (called chunks at 256 MB) are by default roughly compa-rable to HDFS blocks.

In contrast, MapR has no name node at all. Metadata for files and directories is spread across the entire cluster. MapR also has several kinds of data structures that operate at different sizes, with the largest unit being a huge data structure known as a container (30 GB), as depicted in Figure 3-1. There is no equivalent to the container in HDFS. In MapR-FS, the fundamental unit in which files are striped across the cluster is a chunk of configurable size, set by default at 256 MB. The smallest size that can be changed is quite small, 8 kB. The design decision to make blocks small not only enables MapR-FS to allow random updates to files, it also allows MapR-FS to function as a realtime file system, as we discuss in the next section.

All changes to files are reported back to containers, not a name node, and there are containers all over the cluster. This means that meta-data updates are fast, and consequently writers can commit file writes very often and readers can see these updates almost instantly. By split-ting the single HDFS design parameter of block size into three different design parameters of container, chunk, and block sizes that range over nine orders of magnitude, MapR-FS is able to do different things than HDFS can do.

Making Use of a Realtime Distributed File System

Among the prototypical use cases in Chapter 5, we discuss the need for realtime analytics running in a Hadoop-based system. Historically, Hadoop supported parallel computation via a batch compute model known as MapReduce. HDFS, the original Hadoop file system, is well suited to the loads that MapReduce imposes. HDFS, however, is not particularly well suited to direct use by realtime operations. To get around this, data is often stored in memory until a large amount can be flushed at once. This is how HBase works, for instance. Such ap-plications must checkpoint their work rather often, however, to make sure that they can be restarted without data loss.

The point to be made here is that the realtime nature of the MapR file system with its NoSQL database, MapR-DB, changes the response-time parameters that are reasonable goals for projects employing re-altime processing applications. As with any Hadoop distribution, it's important to use Hadoop or NoSQL for the right jobs, but with MapR, subsecond response times without complex workarounds are very much within reach.

Meeting SLAs

When you make guarantees in the form of SLAs for uninterrupted performance, high availability, or fast response times, it is important to make sure that your Hadoop system is well suited for the requirements of the jobs for which you plan to use it. In other words, make sure you are planning to use it for jobs it can do well.

As an example, some MapR customers such as the Aadhaar project mentioned in Chapter 1 are using MapR-DB to store and access data in delay-critical applications. The applications involved often have stringent response time limits. MapR-DB has very tightly constrained response times with no compaction delays. These characteristics make meeting response time SLAs much easier. Systems like HBase are much more difficult to use in these situations because HBase has had to be designed with HDFS limitations in mind and therefore does things like write data in large increments. This can occasionally lead to very long response times. In such situations, the use cases are to some extent MapR specific, not because of any specific feature, but due to predictability. Whatever Hadoop system you are running, you should match its capabilities well to requirements of the particular job of interest in a realistic way in order to be successful.

Deploying Data at Scale to Remote Locations

There are two major reasons to deploy data to remote sites in large-scale systems. One is to make identical data available at multiple processing centers or divisions of a company in different locales. Another purpose is to provide a secondary data center that serves as an off-site duplication of critical data in case of disaster. Both of these needs can be met using MapR's mirroring feature, unique among Hadoop distributions. MapR mirrors are fully consistent incremental copies of data that appear at remote locations atomically. During mirroring, the changes in the data are sent from a source cluster to mirror volumes on the destination cluster. As they arrive, the changes are applied to a snapshot copy of the destination, and when they complete, the snapshot is exposed.

Use cases that depend on mirroring may be possible to implement with HDFS-based Hadoop distributions by simply copying all of the data to the destination machines. If new data can be segregated from old data in specific directories, then this copying can sometimes be set up to avoid excessive data motion. Application cooperation can make sure that partial copies are not processed before they have safely arrived. If this level of management and careful design is an option, then you may be able to achieve similar results without mirroring.

Consistent Data Versioning

MapR's fully consistent snapshots are a specialized feature that makes it possible to have an accurate view of data from an exact point in time. Not only can they be used as a protection against data loss from human error (fat finger syndrome) or software bugs, but consistent snapshots also serve as a means for data versioning. The latter can be particularly useful for preserving an unchanging version of training data for machine learning models or for forensic analysis, in which it is important to be able to demonstrate exactly what was known and when.

HDFS supports a feature called snapshots, but these snapshots are not consistent, nor are they precise. Files that are being updated when a snapshot is made can continue to change after the snapshot is completed. If, however, you arrange to only snapshot directories that have no files being actively changed, then you may be able to use HDFS snapshots (sometimes called fuzzy snapshots) for the same purposes as the atomic and consistent snapshots such as those available with MapR.

Finding the Keys to Success

Now that you have a grounding in how Hadoop works and in the special additional options you may encounter in MapR use cases, let's address the question, "What decisions drive successful Hadoop projects?" In the next chapter we provide a collection of tips drawn from the decisions that have helped to drive success in existing Hadoop and NoSQL projects. Whether you are new to Hadoop or one of the Hadoop pioneers yourself, you may find the advice offered in Chapter 4 is helpful in planning your next step with Hadoop.

Decisions That Drive Successful Hadoop Projects

What are the decisions that drive successful Hadoop projects? The answer lies in part in decisions you make as you plan what project to tackle, the way you design your workflow, and how you've set up your cluster to begin with. Apache Hadoop is a powerful technology that has enormous potential, and the ways in which it can and will be used are still being discovered. Whether you are a seasoned Hadoop user or a newcomer to the technology, there are some key decisions and strategic approaches to using Hadoop for big data systems that can help ensure your own success with Hadoop and related tools, and we offer some suggestions here that may help with your choices.

The following list is not a comprehensive "how-to" guide, nor is it detailed documentation about Hadoop. Instead, it's eclectic. We provide technical and strategic tips—some major and some relatively minor or specialized—that are based on what has helped other Hadoop users succeed. Some of these tips will be helpful before you start using Hadoop, and others are intended for more seasoned users, to guide choices as you put Hadoop to work in development and production settings.

Note that the first three tips are particularly important if you are new to Hadoop and NoSQL databases such as HBase or MapR-DB.

Tip #1: Pick One Thing to Do First

If you work with large volumes of data and need scalability and flexibility, you can use Hadoop in a wide variety of ways to reduce costs, increase revenues, advance your research, and keep you competitive. Adopting Hadoop as your big data platform is a big change from conventional computing, and if you want to be successful quickly, it helps to *focus initially on one specific use for this new technology.*

Don't expect that from the start you can come up with all the different ways that you might eventually want to use Hadoop. Instead, examine your own needs (immediate or long-term goals), pick one need for which Hadoop offers a near-term advantage, and begin planning your initial project. As your team becomes familiar with Hadoop and with the ecosystem tools required for your specific goal, you'll be well positioned to try other things as you see new ways in which Hadoop may be useful to you.

There's no single starting point that's best for everyone. In Chapter 5, we describe some common use cases that fit Hadoop well. Many of those use cases would make reasonable first projects. As you consider what to focus on first, whether it comes from our list or not, make a primary consideration that there is a good match between what you need done and what Hadoop does well. For your first project, don't think about picking the right tool for the job—be a bit opportunistic and pick the right job for the tool.

By focusing on one specific goal to start with, the learning curve for Hadoop and other tools from the ecosystem can be a little less steep. For example, for your first Hadoop project, you might want to pick one with a fairly short development horizon. You can more quickly see whether or not your planning is correct, determine if your architectural flow is effective, and begin to gain familiarity with what Hadoop can do for you. This approach can also get you up and running quickly and let you develop the expertise needed to handle the later, larger, and likely more critical projects.

Many if not most of the successful and large-scale Hadoop users today started with a single highly focused project. That first project led in a natural way to the next project and the next one after that. There is a lot of truth in the saying that big data doesn't cause Hadoop to be installed, but that instead installing Hadoop creates big data. As soon as there is a cluster available, you begin to see the possibilities of work-

---

ing with much larger (and new) datasets. It is amazing to find out how many people had big data projects in their hip pocket and how much value can be gained from bringing them to life.

Tip #2: Shift Your Thinking

Think in a different way so that you change the way that you design systems. This idea of changing how you think may be one of the most important bits of advice we can offer to someone moving from a traditional computing environment into the world of Hadoop. To make this transition of mind may sound trivial, but it actually matters a lot if you are to take full advantage of the potential that Hadoop offers. Here's why.

What we mean by a shift in thinking is that methods and patterns that succeed for large-scale computing are very different from methods and patterns that work in more traditional environments, especially those that involve relational databases and data warehouses. A large-scale shift in thinking is required for the operations, analytics, and applications development teams. *This change is what will let you build systems that make use of what Hadoop does well.* It is undeniably very hard to change the assumptions that are deeply ingrained by years of experience working with traditional systems. The flexibility and innovation of Hadoop systems is a great advantage, but to be fully realized, they must be paired with your own willingness to think in new ways.

Here are a couple of specific examples of how to do this:

- *Learn to delay decisions.* This advice likely feels counterintuitive. We're not advocating procrastination in general—we don't want to encourage bad habits—but it is important to shift your thinking away from the standard idea that you have to design and structure how you will format, transform, and analyze data from the start, before you ingest, store, or analyze any of it.

  This change in thinking is particularly hard to do if you're used to using relational databases, where the application lifecycle of planning, specifying, designing, and implementing can be fairly important and strict. In traditional systems, just how you prepare data (i.e., do ETL) is critically important; you need to choose well before you load, because changing your mind late in the process with a traditional system can be disastrous. That means that with traditional systems such as relational databases, your early decisions really need to be fully and carefully thought through and locked down.

With Hadoop, you don't need to be locked into your first decisions. It's not only unnecessary to narrow your options from the start, it's also not advised. To do so limits too greatly the valuable insights you can unlock through various means of data exploration.

It's not that with Hadoop you should store data without any regard at all for how you plan to use it. Instead, the new idea here is that with Hadoop, the massively lower cost of large-scale data storage and the ability to use a wider variety of data formats means that you can load and use data in relatively raw form, including unstructured or semistructured. In fact, it can be useful to do so because it leaves you open to use it for a known project but also to decide later how else you may want to use the same data. This flexibility is particularly useful since you may use the data for a variety of different projects, some of which you've not yet conceived at the time of data ingestion. The big news is, you're not stuck with your first decisions.

- *Save more data.* If you come from a traditional data storage background, you're probably used to automatically thinking in terms of extracting, transforming, summarizing, and then discarding the raw data. Even where you run analytics on all incoming data for a particular project, you likely do not save more than a few weeks or months of data because the costs of doing so would quickly become prohibitive.

  With Hadoop, that changes dramatically. You can benefit by shifting your thinking to consider saving much longer time spans of your data because data storage can be orders of magnitude less expensive than before. These longer histories can prove valuable to give you a finer-grained view of operations or for retrospective studies such as forensics. Predictive analytics on larger data samples tends to give you a more accurate result. You don't always know what will be of importance in data at the time it is ingested, and the insights that can be gained from a later perspective will not be possible if the pertinent data has already been discarded.

  "Save more data" means saving data for longer time spans, from larger-scale systems, and also from new data sources. Saving data from more sources also opens the way to data exploration—experimental analysis of data alongside your mainstream needs that may unlock surprising new insights. This data exploration is also a reason for delaying decisions about how to process or down-sample data when it is first collected.

Saving data longer can even simplify the basic architecture of system components such as message-queuing systems. Traditional queuing systems worry about deleting messages as soon as the last consumer has acknowledged receipt, but new systems keep messages for a fixed and long time period. If messages that should be processed in seconds will actually persist for a week, the need for fancy acknowledgement mechanisms vanishes. Your architecture may have similar assumptions and similar opportunities.

Tip #3: Start Conservatively But Plan to Expand

A good guideline for your initial purchase of a Hadoop cluster is to start conservatively and then plan to expand at a later date. Don't try to commit to finalizing your cluster size from the start—you'll know more six months down the line about how you want to use Hadoop and therefore what size cluster makes sense than you will when you begin for the first time. Some very rough planning can be helpful just to budget the overall costs of seeing your Hadoop project through to production, but you can make these estimates much better after a bit of experience. Remember, it is fairly easy to expand an initial Hadoop cluster, even by very large factors. To help with that, we provide some tips for successful cluster expansion further along in this list.

That said, make sure to provide yourself with a reasonably sized cluster for your initial development projects. You need to have sufficient computing power and storage capacity to make your first Hadoop project a success, so give it adequate resources. Remember that extra uses for your cluster will pop out of the woodwork almost as soon you get it running. When ideas for new uses arise, be sure to consider whether your initial cluster can handle them or whether it's time to expand. Capacity planning is a key to success.

A common initial cluster configuration as of the writing of this book is 6–12 machines, each with 12–24 disks and 128–192 GB of RAM. If you need to slim this down initially, go for fewer nodes with good specs rather than having more nodes that give very poor performance. If you can swing it, go for 10Gb/s networking.

Tip #4: Be Honest with Yourself

Hadoop offers huge potential cost savings, especially as you scale out wider, because it uses commodity hardware. But it isn't magic. If you set a bad foundation, Hadoop cannot make up for inadequate hardware and setup. If you try to run Hadoop on a couple of poor-quality machines with a few disks and shaky network connections, you won't see very impressive results.

Be honest with yourself about the quality of your hardware and your network connections. Is the disk storage sufficient? Do you have a reasonable balance of cores to disk? Do you have a reasonable balance of CPU and disk capacity for the scale of data storage and analysis you plan to do? And perhaps most important of all, how good are your network connections?

A smoothly running Hadoop cluster will put serious pressure on the disks and network—it's supposed to do so. Make sure each machine can communicate with each other machine at the full bandwidth for your network. Get good-quality switches and be certain that the system is connected properly.

In order to do this, plan time to test your hardware and network connections before you install Hadoop, even if you think that the systems are working fine. That helps you avoid problems or makes it easier to isolate the source of problems if they do arise. If you do not take these preparatory steps and a problem occurs, you won't know if it is hardware or a Hadoop issue that's at fault. Lots of people waste lots of time doing this. In fact, trying to build a high-performance cluster with misconfigured network or disk controllers or memory is common enough that we considered putting it into the chapter on use cases.

The good news is that we have some pointers to good resources for how to test machines for performance. See Appendix A at the end of this book for details.

Tip #5: Plan Ahead for Maintenance

This tip is especially aimed at larger-scale Hadoop users who have expanded to clusters with many machines. Lots of machines in a cluster give you a big boost in computing power, but it also means that in any calendar period, you should expect more maintenance. Many machines means many disks; it's natural that in any few months, some number of them will fail (typical estimates are about 5–8% per year). This is a normal part of the world of large-scale computing (unless you rely solely on cloud computing). It's not a problem, but to have a smoothly running operation, you should build in disk replacement as a regular part of your schedule.

Tip #6: Think Big: Don't Underestimate What You Can (and Will) Want to Do

Hadoop provides some excellent ways to meet some familiar goals, and one of these may be the target of your initial projects when you begin using Hadoop and HBase. In other words, an initial reason to adopt Hadoop is that often it can provide a way to do what you already need to do but in a way that scales better at lower cost. This is a great way to start. It's also likely that as you become familiar with how Hadoop works, you will notice other ways in which it can pay off for you. Some of the ways you choose to expand your use of a Hadoop data system may be new—that's one of the strengths of Hadoop. It not only helps you do familiar things at lower cost, it also unlocks the door to new opportunities.

Stay open to these new possibilities as you go forward; the rewards can surprise you. We see this pattern with people already using Hadoop. A large majority of MapR customers double the size of their clusters in the first year due to increased scope of requirements. What happens is that it quickly becomes apparent that there so many targets of opportunity—unforeseen applications that solve important problems— that additional workload on the clusters quickly justifies additional hardware. It is likely that your experience will be like theirs; your first goals will be fairly straightforward and possibly familiar, but other opportunities will appear quickly. So start relatively small in cluster size, but whatever you do, try not to commit to an absolute upper bound on your final cluster size until you've had a chance to see how Hadoop best fits your needs.

Tip #7: Explore New Data Formats

Some of the most successful decisions we have seen involving Hadoop projects have been to make use of new data formats, including semi-structured or unstructured data. These formats may be unfamiliar to you if you've worked mainly with traditional databases. Some useful new formats such as Parquet or well-known workhorses like JSON allow nested data with very flexible structure. Parquet is a binary data form that allows efficient columnar access, and JSON allows the convenience of a human readable form of data, as displayed in Example 4-1.

Example 4-1. Hadoop enables you to take advantage of nested data formats such as JSON (shown here), thus expanding the number of data sources you can use to gain new insights. Social media sources and web-oriented APIs such as Twitter streams often use JSON. The new open source SQL-on-Hadoop query engine Apache Drill is able to query nested data structures in either JSON or Parquet. See Ford VIN Decoder (http://www.fleet.ford.com/maintenance/vin-decoder/) for more information.

```
{
    "VIN":"3FAFW33407M000098",
    "manufacturer":"Ford",
    "model": {
      "base": "Ford F-Series, F-350",
      "options": [
        "Crew Cab", "4WD", "Dual Rear Wheels"
      ]
    },
    "engine":{
      "class": "V6,Essex",
      "displacement": "3.8 L",
      "misc": ["EFI","Gasoline","190hp"]
    },
    "year":2007
}
```

Nested data provides you with some interesting new options. Think of it as you would this book—the book is an analogy for nested data. It's one thing, but it contains subsets of content at different levels, such as chapters, figure legends, and individual sentences. Nested data can be treated as a unit, but with the right access, the data at each internal layer can be used.

Nested data formats such as Parquet combine flexibility with performance. A key benefit of this flexibility is that it allows you to "future-proof" your applications. Old applications will silently ignore new data fields, and new applications can still read old data. Combined with a little bit of discipline, these methods lead to very flexible interfaces. This style of data structure migration was pioneered by Google and has proved very successful in a wide range of companies.

Besides future-proofing, nested data formats let you encapsulate structures. Just as with programming languages, encapsulation allows data to be more understandable and allows you to hide irrelevant details.

These new formats seem very strange at first if you come from a relational data background, but they quickly become second nature if you give them a try. One of your challenges for success is to encourage your teams to begin to consider unstructured and semistructured data among their options. What all this means from a business perspective is that access to semistructured, unstructured, and nested data formats greatly expand your chances to reap the benefits of analyzing social data, of combining insights from diverse sources, and reducing development time through more efficient workflows for some projects.

Tip #8: Consider Data Placement When You Expand a Cluster

Having just recommended (in "Tip #3: Start Conservatively But Plan to Expand" on page 33) that you start small and expand your cluster as you understand your workload, we should also suggest that some care is in order when you do expand a cluster, especially if you expand a heavily loaded cluster just by a small amount. This situation is a very common use case because it often happens that usage of a new cluster expands far more quickly than planned, and people may initially choose to upgrade by adding only a few additional nodes. The challenge can arise because new data will tend to be loaded onto the newly available and more empty new nodes unless you take measures to regulate what happens. Figure 4-1 shows what can happen if you start with five very full nodes and add two new ones.

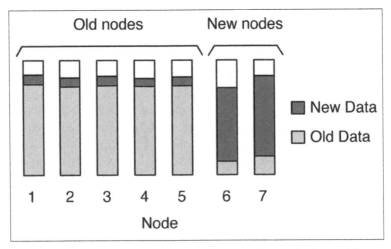

Figure 4-1. An odd effect that is sometimes observed when adding a few nodes to a nearly full cluster. New data (shown here in red) can become unevenly distributed across the cluster. If new data is hotter than old data, this focus on new data on new nodes will make them hotter as well—it's as though for a subset of operations, the cluster has the appearance of being smaller than before. In that case, adding just a few new machines to the cluster can inadvertently decrease current cluster throughput.

Tip #9: Plot Your Expansion

The advice here is really simple: Don't wait until your cluster is almost full before you decide to expand, particularly if you are not working in the cloud. Instead, plan ahead to include sufficient time for ordering new hardware and getting it delivered, set up, and pretested before you install your Hadoop software and begin to ingest data.

To do this capacity planning well, you will need to estimate not only how long it will take from decision to order to having up-and-running machines, you also will need to estimate growth rates for your system and set a target threshold (e.g., 70% of capacity used) as the alert to start the expansion process. You can measure and record machine loads, probably using a time series database, and plot your rate of decrease in available space. That lets you more easily incorporate an appropriate lead time when you order new hardware in order to avoid crunches.

Tip #10: Form a Queue to the Right, Please

When you are dealing with streaming data, it makes good sense to plan a queuing step as part of data ingestion to the Hadoop cluster or for the output of a realtime analytics application in your project architecture. If there is any interruption of the processing of streaming data due to application error, software upgrades, traffic problems, or cosmic rays, losing data is usually less acceptable than delayed processing. A queuing layer lets you go back and pick up where your process left off once the data processing can resume. Some data sources inherently incorporate replayable queues, but many do not. Especially for data sources that are non-local, queuing is just a very good idea.

As mentioned in our overview of the Hadoop ecosystem presented in Chapter 2, there are several useful tools for providing the safety of a queue for streaming data. Apache Kafka is particularly useful for this purpose.

Tip #11: Provide Reliable Primary Persistence When Using Search Tools

As powerful and useful as they are, search tools are not suitable as primary data stores, although it may be tempting to think of them that way when you are storing data in them. Successful projects are planned with built-in protections, and one aspect of that planning is to respect search technologies such as ElasticSearch for what they do well but not to assume that they provide a dependable primary data store. They were not designed to do so, and trying use them for that purpose can result in data loss or substantial performance loss.

The alternative is safe and easy: archive data in your Hadoop system as the primary store rather than relying on what is stored in the search tool. With the low cost of data storage in Hadoop systems, there isn't a big penalty for persisting data for primary storage in Hadoop rather than relying on your search engine. In terms of protecting data, there are big benefits for doing so.

Tip #12: Establish Remote Clusters for Disaster Recovery

Your initial Hadoop project may not be business critical, but there is a good chance that a business-critical application will be on your cluster by at least the end of the first year of production. Even if the processing isn't business critical, data retention may well be. Before that happens, you will need to think through how to deal with the unlikely but potentially devastating effects of a disaster. For small startups, the answer might be that it is better to roll the dice to avoid the distraction and cost of a second data center, but that is rarely an option with an established business.

If you have data of significant value and applications that run in critical-path operations for your organization, it makes sense to plan ahead for data protection and recovery in case of a disaster such as fire, flood, or network access failure in a data center. The remote mirroring capabilities of MapR make it possible to do this preparation for disaster recovery (DR) even for very large-scale systems in a reliable, fast, and convenient way using remote mirroring.

Chapter 3 explains more about how MapR mirroring works. Keep in mind that once remote mirroring is established, only the incremental differences in data files are transmitted, rather than complete new copies. Compression of this data differential for transfer to the remote cluster makes the process fast and keeps bandwidth costs down. There is no observable performance penalty and each completed mirror will atomically advance to a consistent state of the mirror source.

Mirrors like this are a MapR-specific feature. What are your options for DR in other Hadoop distributions? On HDFS-based systems, you can use the built-in distributed copy (`distcp`) utility to copy entire directory trees between clusters. This utility can make copies appear nearly atomically, but it doesn't have any way to do a true incremental copy. When `distcp` is used in production, it is common for it to be combined with conventions so that files that are currently being modified are segregated into a separate directory tree. Once no more modifications are being made to this directory tree and a new live tree is created, the copy to the remote cluster can be initiated.

One thing to keep in mind is that a DR cluster is not entirely a waste of resources in the absence of a disaster. Such a backup cluster can be used as a development sandbox or staging environment. If you have frequent data synchronization and can protect the backup data from inadvertent modification, this can be a very fruitful strategy.

Tip #13: Take a Complete View of Performance

Performance is not only about who wins a sprint. Sometimes the race is a marathon. Or the goal is to throw a javelin. The key is to know which event you are competing in. The same is true with Hadoop clusters.

Too often, an organization assesses which tool they want to adopt just by comparing how fast each one completes running a single specific job or query. Speed is important, and benchmark speeds like this can be informative, but the speed on a small set of queries is only a small part of the picture in terms of what may matter most to success in your particular project. Another consideration is long-term throughput: which tool has stayed up and running and therefore supported the most work two weeks or two months later?

Performance quality should also be judged relative to the needs of the particular project. As mentioned briefly in Chapter 2, what's most commonly important as a figure of merit in streaming and realtime analytics is latency (the time from arrival of a record to completion of the processing for that record). In contrast, for interactive processing, the data remains fixed and the time of interest is the time that elapses between presenting a query and getting a result—in other words, the response time.

In each of these situations, a measure of performance can be helpful in picking the right tool and the right workflow for the job, but you must be careful that you're measuring the right form of performance.

Once you have picked key performance indicators for the applications you are running, it is just as important to actually measure these indicators continuously and record the results. Having a history of how a particular job has run over time is an excellent diagnostic for determining if there are issues with the cluster, possibly due to hardware problems, overloading from rogue processes, or other issues.

Another very useful trick is to define special "canary" jobs that have constant inputs and that run the same way each time. Since their inputs are constant and since they are run with the same resources each time they are run, their performance should be comparable each time they are run. If their performance changes, something may have happened to the cluster. With streaming environments, such tests are usually conducted by putting special records known as "tracer bullets" into the system. The processing of tracers triggers additional logging and diagnostics, and the results are used very much like the performance of canary jobs.

Tip #14: Read Our Other Books (Really!)

We've written several short books published by O'Reilly that provide pointers to handy ways to build Hadoop applications for practical machine learning, such as how to do more effective anomaly detection (*Practical Machine Learning: A New Look at Anomaly Detection* (*http://bit.ly/anomaly_detection*)), how to build a simple but very powerful recommendation engine (*Practical Machine Learning: Innovations in Recommendation* (*http://oreil.ly/1qt7riC*)), and how to build high-performance time series databases (*Time Series Databases: New Ways to Store and Access Data* (*http://oreil.ly/1ulZnOf*)). Each of these short books takes on a single use case and elaborates on the most important aspects of that use case in an approachable way. In our current book, we are doing the opposite, treating many use cases at a considerably lower level of detail. Both approaches are useful.

So check those other books out—you may find lots of good tips that fit your project.

Tip # 15: Just Do It

Hadoop offers practical, cost-effective benefits right now, but it's also about innovation and preparing for the future. One decision with large potential payoffs is to get up to speed now with new technologies before the need for them is absolutely critical. This gives you time to gain familiarity, to fit the way a tool is used to your own specific needs, and to build your organization's foundation of expertise with new approaches before you are pressed against an extreme deadline.

The only way to gain this familiarity is to pick a project and just do it!

CHAPTER 5

Prototypical Hadoop Use Cases

In this chapter, we present a collection of some of the most appealing use cases when considering what Hadoop might do for you. These are prototypical use cases—isolated goals and the Hadoop-based solutions that address them. They are not theoretical. They come from observations of some of the most common and most rewarding ways in which Hadoop is being used, including showing its value in large-scale production systems. We identify each use case by the major intent of its design, to make it easier for you to extrapolate to your own needs. Then, in Chapter 6, we will tell some real-world stories about how MapR customers have combined these use cases to put Hadoop to work.

Data Warehouse Optimization

One of the most straightforward ways to use Hadoop to immediate advantage is to employ it for optimization of your use of a costly data warehouse. The goal of data warehouse (DW) optimization is to make the best use of your data warehouse (or relational database) resources in order to lower costs and keep your data warehouse working efficiently as your data scales up. One way to do this that offers a big payback is to move early ETL processing and staging tables off of the data warehouse onto a Hadoop cluster for processing. This approach is advantageous because these ETL steps often consume the majority of the processing power of the data warehouse, but they only constitute a much smaller fraction of the total lines of code. Moreover, the staging tables that are inputs to these ETL steps are typically much larger than subsequent tables, so moving these tables to Hadoop can result in substantial space savings. You gain an advantage by relieving strain on the data warehouse at your current data volumes, plus you'll have set up a highly scalable system that will continue to work in a cost-effective way even as data volumes grow enormously. It makes sense to move each part of the process to the platform on which it works most efficiently. Often initial data ingestion and ETL makes sense on Hadoop, while it may make sense to keep critical-path traditional processes on the data warehouse as before.

Figure 5-1 shows the evolution of a data warehouse system as data warehouse optimization proceeds. Initially, in the top panel, we see the traditional view of the process. Data is ingested by copying it into a shared storage device such as a network attached storage system (NAS). This data is then imported into the staging tables on the actual data warehouse, and important data is extracted and transformed before loading (ETL) and final processing. This use of staging tables is broadly like what we have seen in actual customer installations. Significantly, the majority of computational resources are typically consumed in the ETL processing, but only a small minority of the code complexity is in this phase.

This process can be changed by using your Hadoop platform to optimize the system, as shown in the bottom two panels of Figure 5-1. In the middle panel of the figure, we see how this optimization works on the Hadoop platform from MapR. Here, data is copied from the original source to an NFS-mounted file system exactly as before, but now the NAS has been replaced by a MapR cluster that holds the staging tables. All or some of the ETL process is run on the Hadoop cluster instead of the data warehouse, and then the work product of the ETL process is bulk loaded into the data warehouse using standard bulk import tools via another NFS mount of the Hadoop cluster.

The lower panel of Figure 5-1 shows an alternative design for non-MapR Hadoop platforms. The goal is the same, but there are some variations in how the data is ingested for ETL and how the refined data is exported to the data warehouse. The biggest difference is the use of specialized connectors to work around the lack of high-performance NFS access to the HDFS cluster.

Exactly how much of the ETL process is moved to the Hadoop cluster depends on the exact trade-off of code size, performance, and natural modularity in the code on the data warehouse. Typically, true extract and transform code runs much more efficiently on a Hadoop cluster than a data warehouse, while advanced reporting code may run faster on the data warehouse. These speed trade-offs have to be measured empirically by converting sample queries, and the benefits of conversion then have to be balanced against fixed conversion costs and the variable costs of running the process on the Hadoop cluster. The final reporting code on the data warehouse is often large enough, complex enough, and difficult enough to test that the trade-off is clearly on the side of leaving it in place, at least initially.

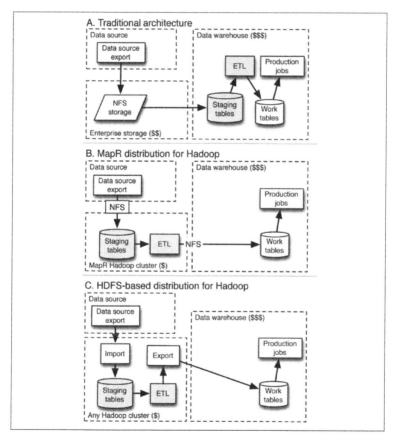

Figure 5-1. Data warehouse optimization works by moving staging tables and ETL processing to a Hadoop cluster, as shown in panels B and C. This change eliminates the need for a storage appliance to facilitate the transfer and removes considerable processing and storage load from the data warehouse.

Optimization can be done with any kind of Hadoop cluster by using special-purpose connectors as shown in the bottom panel (c) of Figure 5-1. With a MapR cluster (b), the need for connectors is avoided by using standard bulk export and bulk import utilities on the data source and data warehouse systems respectively together with NFS access to the MapR cluster.

The savings in using a Hadoop platform for DW optimization come from the displacement of the external storage and the substantial decrease in table space and ETL processing required on the data warehouse. This is offset slightly by the cost of the Hadoop cluster, but the net result is usually a substantial savings. In some cases, these savings are realized by the need for a smaller data warehouse, in others by a delay in having to upgrade or expand an existing data warehouse. In addition to a cost advantage, this style of Hadoop-based DW optimization keeps all parts of the process running efficiently as your system grows. The move to Hadoop therefore future-proofs your architecture.

Data Hub

A significant fraction of MapR customers name the centralization of data—sometimes called a data hub or data lake—as one of the most important Hadoop use cases. The terms are loosely defined, but the centralization concept is fairly simple and very powerful: by bringing together data from a variety of sources and data types (structured, unstructured, or semistructured, including nested data) into a centralized storage accessible by many different groups for various types of analysis or export to other systems, you widen the possibilities for what insights you can harvest.

The concept of an enterprise data hub illustrates some key emerging trends for Hadoop clusters. The most important such trend is that Hadoop clusters are becoming less and less specialized and more and more a company-wide resource. This is particularly good because it means the potential peak computing capacity an application can access is larger than would be possible with isolated clusters. In addition, the centralization of data helps break down unwanted data silos. Some forms of analysis, including some valuable approaches to machine learning, are greatly improved by being able to combine insights from more than one data source.

The data hub is a natural evolution from the data warehouse optimization use case as well. Because the early stages of ETL bring in and persist raw data onto the Hadoop cluster, that same data can be accessed for other purposes, which can lead organically to the construction of a data hub. The relatively low cost of large-scale storage on Hadoop makes this particularly attractive. Remember "Tip #2: Shift Your Thinking" on page 31 in Chapter 4 that referred to the benefit of delaying some decisions about how you want to process and use data? The data hub fits that idea by building a central source in which data can be used in a variety of ways for many different internal customers, some currently of interest, others to be discovered in the future, as depicted in Figure 5-2.

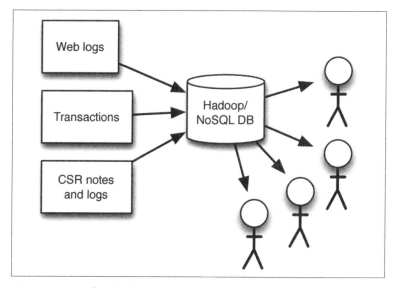

Figure 5-2. A data hub centralizes data from many sources and provides access to many users, such as different groups of developers, data scientists, and business analysts. Here the reference database would be NoSQL HBase or MapR-DB. Having easy access to widely varied data makes new ideas and applications inevitable.

A data hub on a Hadoop cluster may support development of a customer 360 database, as described in the next section, along with ETL for data warehouse optimization, analysis of log data, processing of streaming data to be visualized on a dashboard, complex anomaly detection, other machine learning projects, and more. The common theme is that these clusters have a lot going on on them in all kinds of ways.

Customer 360

The goal of a customer 360 system is to establish a high-performance, consolidated store of complete histories for every customer. When this is done and the entire history for a single customer is viewed as a single consistent list of events, many kinds of processing become enormously simpler. The basic idea is that the non-relational, highly flexible nature of state-of-the-art big data allows dramatically simpler interpretation of the data without having to join hundreds of tables from incompatible snowflake schemas together.

The idealized view of one data store to rule them all often gives way a bit to a structure more like the one shown in Figure 5-3. Here, as in the idealized view, many data sources are concentrated into a central store. These streams are accumulated in a reference database that is keyed by a common customer identifier. The records in these streams are nearly or fully denormalized so that they can cross from one machine to another, maintaining their internal consistency and integrity.

This reference database is stored in a NoSQL database such as HBase or MapR-DB. The key advantage that these databases offer for an application like this is that good key design will allow all of the records for any single customer to be stored nearly contiguously on disk. This means that a single customer's data can be read very quickly—so fast, indeed, that the inherent expansion in the data caused by denormalization can often be more than compensated by the speed advantage of contiguous reads.

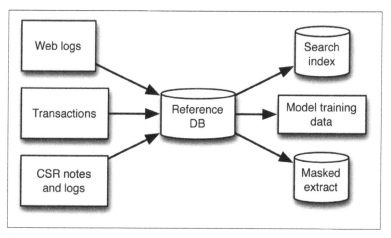

Figure 5-3. In a customer 360 system, all kinds of information for a single customer is collected into a reference database and kept in a way so that customer histories can be accessed very quickly and with comprehensive retrieval of all desired data. In practice, internal customers of the data have specialized enough needs that it pays to extract views of the reference database into smaller, special-purpose sub-databases.

When building a customer 360 database like this, it is likely that you will quickly find that your internal customers of this data will need specialized access to the data. For instance, one common requirement is to be able to search for patterns in the customer histories using a search engine. Search engines like ElasticSearch fill the requirement for search, but they are not rated for use as a primary data store, as we mentioned in "Tip #11: Provide Reliable Primary Persistence When Using Search Tools" on page 39 in Chapter 4. The easy middle ground is to replicate a filtered extract of the updates to the main database to the search engine in near-real time. This near-real time replication can be easily implemented in both MapR-DB and in HBase. Forthcoming releases of MapR-DB will have a specialized asynchronous mirroring capability that will make this operation even easier.

Another important consumer of customer 360 data might be a team of machine learning experts building a predictive model. These teams typically prefer no database at all, but rather prefer to get data in flat files. A common way to deal with this requirement is to run periodic extracts from the main database to get the record set that the team needs into a flat file and then, on a MapR system, to use mirroring to deploy the file or files to the cluster the machine learning team is using. This method isolates the unpredictable machine load of the machine learning software from the production environment for the reference database. The use of programs like rsync to update the actual mirrored data on the master machine can allow the mirroring update to move far less data than a full copy.

Transactionally correct mirroring is not available on HDFS-based versions of Hadoop, however, so a workaround is required on these other Hadoop systems to allow this type of data delivery. The typical approach used on non-MapR systems is to invoke a MapReduce program called distcp to copy the files to the development cluster. Careful management is required to avoid changing the files and directories being copied during the copy, but this alternative approach can make the customer 360 use case work on these other Hadoop systems, too.

Another common reason for custom extracts is to comply with security standards. The reference database typically contains sensitive information, possibly in encrypted or masked form. Permission schemes on columns in the reference database are used to enforce role-based limitations on who can access data in the database. Different versions of sensitive information are likely stored in different columns to give flexibility in terms of what data people can see. In order to secure the sensitive information in the reference database even more stringently, it is common to produce special versions of the reference database with all sensitive data masked or even omitted. Such an extract can be manipulated much more freely than the original and can be hosted on machines with lower security profiles, making management and access easier. Security-cleared extracts like this may be more useful even than the original data for many applications.

Recommendation Engine

The motivation for building a recommendation engine generally is to improve customer experience by better understanding what will appeal to particular customers based on the preferences communicated through their actions. This improved experience can result in increased sales, longer retention for services, stickier websites, or higher efficiency for marketing spend. In short, happier customers generally result in improved business.

Hadoop provides an excellent platform for building and deploying a recommendation system, particularly because good recommendation requires very large datasets to train a model. A simple but very powerful recommender can be built and deployed easily by exploiting search technology running on a Hadoop platform. Let's take a look at how that works.

The goal of a recommendation engine is to present customers with opportunities that they might not otherwise find by normal browsing and searching. This is done by using historical user behavior for the entire population of users to find patterns that are then cross-referenced to the recent behavior of a specific user. Recommendations can be presented to users explicitly in the form of a list of recommended items or offers, but can also be used more subtly to make a user's overall experience more relevant to what they want to do. As an example, a "What's new" page could literally just show new items in reverse chronological order of introduction, or it could show all items introduced recently ordered by a recommendation engine. The latter approach tends to engage users more strongly.

Recommendation systems work by reading large amounts of historical data and doing a large analysis. This analysis is typically run as a batch or offline process since it may take tens of minutes to hours to run. The output of the analysis consists of so-called recommendation indicators and is transferred to a system that can match these indicators to recent behavior of a specific user to make recommendations in real time as soon as new behavior is observed. The system that makes these realtime recommendations can be implemented using a search engine. This implementation choice is very convenient since search engines are often already being used. Another advantage of this design for recommendation is that the more computationally expensive and time-consuming part of the project, building and training the recommendation model, is done offline, ahead of time, allowing recommendations to be made for users in real time, online, as outlined in Figure 5-4.

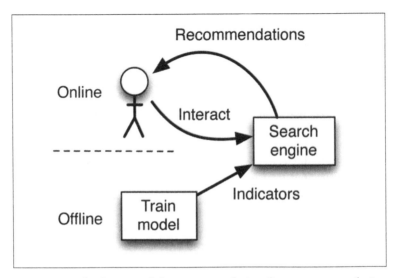

Figure 5-4. The beauty of this two-part design for a recommendation engine is that by dividing the computation of recommendations into two parts, most of the computation can be done offline. That offline computation prepares information called indicators that a standard search engine can use to deliver customized recommendations in real time.

The offline part of the computation is shown in Figure 5-5. User behavioral history is analyzed both for *co-occurrence* of behavior and for cross-occurrence. In co-occurrence, behaviors are compared like-to-like. An example might be that if you want to recommend songs to a listener, you would analyze previous song-listening behavior. To recommend books for purchase, you would analyze previous book purchases. With cross-occurrence, in contrast, you would analyze past behavior of one type to make recommendations of a different type. An example would be using past behavior consisting of reading reviews for a product to recommend purchase of that item or others. Using multiple cross-occurrences together with co-occurrence is a valuable way to improve recommender performance.

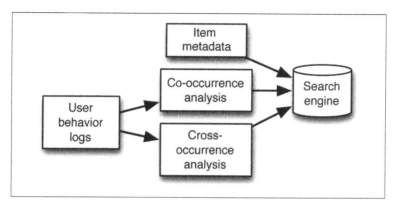

Figure 5-5. This figure shows a rough structure for the offline portion of a recommendation analysis system. Historical behavior is recorded in user behavior logs. These logs are examined to generate recommendation indicators by doing co-occurrence and cross-occurrence analysis. These indicators are inserted into a search engine together with conventional item metadata that would normally have been in the search engine.

You can find more information on how recommendation engines are built in our previous book, *Practical Machine Learning: Innovations in Recommendation (http://oreil.ly/1qt7riC)*. The book provides a very short introduction into how to build a recommendation engine and describes the theory and basic practice.

Marketing Optimization

The goal of marketing optimization is to understand what causes customers to ultimately buy products across both marketing and sales cycles. In very few businesses, the things that get customers to engage with a company and the sales process that ensues are relatively simple. An example might be a web-only company that has only a few online marketing programs. In contrast, many businesses are at the other extreme and have a large number of marketing contacts with customers, and the sales process consists of many interactions as well. For businesses with anything but the simplest sales cycles, determining which actions actually help sell things to customers and which things either don't help or even impede sales is both hard and very important. In some cases, a company has enough products that just deciding which products to talk about at which times can make a significant difference to the business.

The best practice for this problem is to first establish as complete a history of interactions with customers as possible. Typically, this takes the form of some kind of customer 360 database. The simplest marketing optimization system and usually the first one implemented is a recommendation system of some kind. The goal here is to recognize which customers are likely to be in a position where offering a particular product to them is likely to result in a sale or other desired response.

Recommendation systems are very common in online business, but it is unusual to integrate online and offline experiences as inputs to a recommender, and it is unusual to drive recommendations uniformly to both online and offline customer interactions.

The next step in complexity beyond an indicator-based recommendation system is to build per-product sales models. These models can use behavioral features, including recommendation indicators and detailed timing of past transactions and marketing efforts, to attempt to guide the direct sales process by determining which products have the highest propensity to sell if pitched. These models are more complex than the models implicit in a normal recommender, and building them is likely to take a considerable amount of computation, but for complex sales cycles, the results can be very significant. The level of effort to build these models, however, is substantial and should only be undertaken if the product line and sales cycle justify the additional complexity. Simpler search engine–based recommenders are much more appropriate for many companies, including most business-to-consumer companies, both because the sales cycle tends to be simpler, but also because spending time on complex machine learning development is probably only worth it if there is sufficient leverage to reward the development. Extreme sales volume is one way to provide this leverage; high per-unit net profit is another way. For companies that don't have these factors, it is often much more valuable to spend time adding more logging to user interactions and tuning the user experience to better incorporate recommendations from simpler recommendation systems instead.

Large Object Store

The goal of a large object store is to store a large number of data objects that need to be accessed individually, often by name, but that are not necessarily of interest for wholesale analysis. In terms of how the objects in an object store are thought of, a large object store would be very nicely persisted in individual flat files, one per object, rather than a database. This is particularly true because the objects are often relatively large, often over a megabyte on average. Often the underlying purpose for a large object store is to provide access to media such as videos or audio recordings; sometimes the objects have to do with messaging systems or systems data. Typically, the number of objects is in the tens of millions to tens of billions, and the sizes of the objects involved range from tens of kilobytes to hundreds of megabytes. One common requirement is that objects be accessible on the web. Downtime is typically unacceptable in these systems, and 99.9th percentile response, exclusive of transmission time, must typically be in the tens of milliseconds.

Objects in systems like this often come from a very large number of Internet-connected devices. These devices are often the primary consumer of these objects, but large scans of objects are common requirements as well. For instance, if you are building a video serving site on a large object store, it will occasionally be necessary to transcode files into new formats or to extract thumbnail images or run image classifiers. In media systems, the total number of files is typically much larger than the number of individual videos being served because of the requirement to have multiple encoding formats at multiple bit rates along with additional media assets like thumbnail images and preview clips. A good rule of thumb is to expect roughly 100 times more files than you have conceptual objects such as a video.

Traditionally, large object stores have been built on top of special storage hardware at very high cost, or purpose built using a combination of databases (to store object locations) and conventional file systems at very high cost in operational complexity.

Hadoop systems can be used to build large object stores very nicely. With a MapR system, you can simply use the system as a very large file system since the very large number of files and their large size are not a problem for MapR-FS. Using NFS to allow direct access by conventional web services also works well with such a solution.

With an HDFS-based system, a completely file-oriented implementation will only work at moderate to small scale due to the file count limit that comes from the basic architecture of HDFS. Depending on the file size distribution, you may be able to use a combination of HBase to store smaller files and HDFS to store larger files. All of the HDFS-based solutions require special software to translate requests into the HDFS API.

Log Processing

Large computing systems are composed of processes that transform data (as in ETL processes) or respond to queries (as with databases or web servers), but all of these programs typically annotate the actions they take or the anomalous conditions they encounter as so-called log events, which are stored in log files. There's a wealth of insights to be drawn from log file data, but up until recently, much of it has been overlooked and discarded. Logs can be used to trigger alerts, monitor the current state of your machines, or to diagnose a problem shortly after it happens, but traditionally, the data has not been saved for more than a short period of time.

These log events often record a huge range of observations, such as records of performance or breakage. These records can capture the footprints of intruders or provide a detailed view of a customer's online behavior. Yet when system diagrams are drawn, these logs are rarely shown. In fact, some people refer to log files as "data exhaust" as though they are just expendable and unwanted pollution. Traditionally, logs were deleted shortly after being recorded, but even if retained, they were difficult to process due to their size. That is changing. Hadoop makes it possible to store and process log data because it allows cheap and scalable data storage and the ability to process large amounts of data.

Traditionally, log processing has been done by arranging an intricate dance between the producers of these logs and the programs that analyze the logs. On the producer side, the tradition has been to "roll" the logs by closing one log file when it reaches an age or size constraint, then start writing to another. As log files are closed, they become available for transport to the analysis program. On the receiving side, this dance was mirrored by methods for signaling exactly which files were to be processed and when programs were to run. Moreover, the output of one process typically was input to another, so this signaling dance cascaded.

This sort of processing can work well enough when all is well, but havoc reigns when something breaks or even when something is substantially delayed. Questions about whether old results had to be recomputed and which programs needed to be run late or run again were very difficult to answer.

In order to fill the need to control these log processing programs, some intricate frameworks have been developed. In the Hadoop world, these include Apache Flume and Apache Oozie. Unfortunately, the goal of these frameworks is to manage the complexity of log processing, not to radically simplify it.

More recently, a new pattern has emerged in which log processing is unified around a queuing system. The use of a message-queuing style dramatically simplifies the issues of what to do when and how to redo work that is affected by late-arriving data or system failures. This new pattern of processing has proven dramatically better than the old file-shipping style of log analysis and is the primary topic of the next section on realtime analytics. For log analytics, we recommend that you use Hadoop and that you jump into the new style with both feet.

Realtime Analytics

The goal of realtime analytics is to analyze a sequence of records in near-real time, allowing models to produce alerts or update status displays soon after data arrives. This can be used for log processing, but also for processing many other kinds of streams of records. The business goal of such processing is primarily to react to events quickly, but a major secondary benefit is to establish uniformity in how records are processed to lower the cost of developing analytics programs. This style of processing can be used for the analysis of very general kinds of transactions, but it has been especially popular in the analysis of system logs, particularly those that have to do with security. That is not to say that the use case described here is intended to replace existing security analytics tools. Instead, the log analytics techniques described here complement these other tools by allowing more variety in the logs being analyzed and the retention of logs for analysis over much longer time periods.

Of particular interest in the context of this book is that Hadoop provides an excellent foundation for this style of processing. To understand why and how the current best practice architectures for realtime analytics have come about, especially analytics based on log events, it helps a bit to look back to where log analytics came from. Not all that long ago, a lot of systems looked roughly like the diagram shown in Figure 5-6. Typically starting with a single server, log files were accumulated to get very rough estimates of daily traffic. There was no question about which format the servers used to log events, and there was no question about what format the accumulation program used. They both used *the* format.

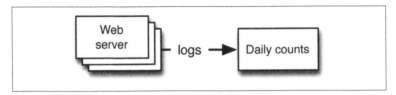

Figure 5-6. Not so very long ago, log analytics worked a lot like this. Web servers recorded events in logs and very simple aggregation programs totaled these events up each day.

This somewhat exaggerated halcyon period of simplicity quickly gave way to a cacophony of different systems recording new kinds of data in new formats that had to be analyzed more quickly and in more ways than before. Moving logs from each source to each analysis became very complex and the analysis programs outgrew the available resources. Figure 5-7 shows how complexity creeps into this. Solutions to the problems that arose were often patchwork solutions produced ad hoc as the problems were recognized.

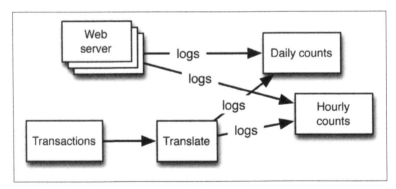

Figure 5-7. The problem: the simplicity of systems such as the one shown in Figure 5-6 quickly gave way to increased numbers of data sources, an explosion in data formats, and a multiplicity of new analysis requirements. A better approach that unifies processing is needed.

In a modern analytics workflow, things have become a bit simpler again. The reason for this simplification is the insertion of a message-queuing system into the heart of the system that is charged with moving all of the log-like information from producers to consumers of the information. Some systems are sources of data and some are sinks. Others consume data only to transform it and inject it back into the queuing system. Some data streams have many consumers. Others only one (or even none). The point of the architecture is that data flows in relatively uniform formats through a uniform interface. The queuing system acts as a sort of a post office where anyone needing access to live data can go to fetch the data. Having a consistent and universal method of moving log-like data makes the overall system vastly simpler to reason about and to build.

Apache Kafka is one of the popular choices for such a queuing system, largely because it provides an extremely simple model of operation that in turn enables very reliable operation at very high throughputs. In such a system, log files are ingested in a data stream known as a topic. Extraction or transformation programs can read messages from a topic and send the results to other topics. Archive programs can read from any topic and store a history of the messages found under that topic to flat files or databases for later interactive analysis. Other programs can read messages in topics and do realtime analysis on them, putting the results of the analysis into a result database or back into yet another queue. An overall architecture of such a system is shown in Figure 5-8.

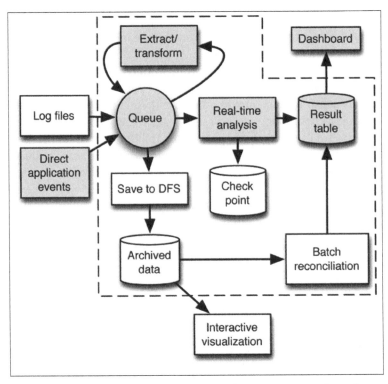

Figure 5-8. A queuing system adds a key function to a Hadoop cluster to provide reliable message streaming from component to component in the realtime analytics system. Programs can process records and then save the results to the distributed file system in the cluster or send the results back into another message stream. Realtime analysis is possible and can be combined with batch or interactive analysis relatively easily. In this diagram, the shaded blocks are the realtime path, while unshaded blocks run as batch. Blocks inside the dashed lines can be implemented on a MapR cluster. For an HDFS-based cluster, the queue can be implemented using Kafka.

Most or all of the components in such a realtime analysis network will not only produce results, but they also throw off a considerable amount of diagnostic information about what they are doing and how they are functioning. This diagnostic information can be in the form of log events that can be analyzed in real time by the same realtime log analysis system or as time series data to be inserted into a time series database.

The use of batch reconciliation programs that run periodically and overwrite the results of the realtime components of a system is also a common pattern. The idea is that it is very difficult to make the real-time components of the system (a) reliable in the face of potentially bizarre malfunctions, (b) absolutely correct in all their outputs, and (c) very fast. At large scale, allowing scalability, performance, reliability, and/or availability of the system to trump considerations of absolute accuracy in the short term can be a very valuable strategy. In such cases, it is often relatively easy to build batch programs that reprocess the archived data in order to ensure that correctness is eventually added to the qualities of the system. The use of a reconciliation process in this way is the primary feature of what is known as the lambda architecture, as mentioned previously.

It should be noted that while this design involves message passing as the dominant form of data transfer, there is a world of difference from what is normally called message bus architecture or enterprise service bus. The difference stems from the fact that Kafka-like systems do not remember whether messages have been delivered or not. There is no effort on the part of Kafka to ensure delivery of every message exactly once to every consumer of the message. Instead, what Kafka does is ride the wave of massively lower storage costs by simply keeping messages for a much longer period of time than is expected for the processing of the messages. Messages that are typically processed in seconds might be kept for days. The proximate effect of this retention is that if processing of a message fails to happen, the message can almost certainly be re-read after the condition that caused the failure has been repaired. This fact, in turn, allows Kafka clients to take control over deciding which messages have been read and processed, and that allows Kafka to be vastly simpler and much faster.

The results in companies that we have seen using Kafka as a nearly universal means of transporting stream-oriented data have been uniformly good. As such, we recommend that this style be the way that streaming data or log files be processed if possible.

Time Series Database

Interest in time series data is becoming much more widespread as people increasingly see the value in collecting and analyzing machine data from servers and from a wide variety of sensors such as those involved in the Internet of Things. As a result, it's important to have a way to build a reliable, high-performance time series database. A Hadoop-based NoSQL solution such as Apache HBase or MapR-DB is a great way to do this.

The goal of a time series database is to store a large mass of historical measurements from many sensors, each associated with the time that the measurement was made and to allow rapid retrieval from such a database. These sensors may actually be implemented in software to make measurements such as how long it takes to process a single record or how much data is stored on a disk, but they are also commonly real sensors making measurements of tangible, physical phenomena such as temperatures, flow rates, or vibration.

Time series data can be stored in a conventional database, but as the volume of measurement gets larger, the aggregate number of measurements per second gets higher and the required retrieval rates increase, a conventional database will break down. As a result, only a short time frame of data can be saved, and even this is not optimal on a relational database. The problem is that for this particular restricted application, conventional databases provide more capabilities than are required, and those additional capabilities are costly even if not used.

NoSQL databases such as MapR-DB or HBase, when paired with appropriate time series software, can store and retrieve time series data at much higher rates than a conventional database, and the rate at which they can process data can be scaled up or down easily by adding or removing computers for the task. Figure 5-9 shows schematically how data sources feed a time series database and how the contents of the database are viewed and analyzed.

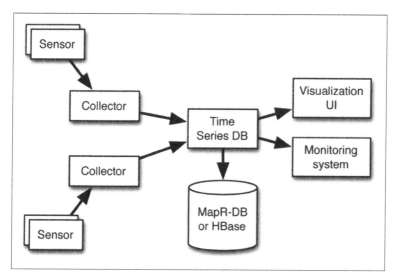

Figure 5-9. Collector programs read data from sensors, either virtual or physical, and the measurements to the time series database that stores the data in MapR-DB or HBase. The data in the database is arranged so that it can be read back quickly in large volumes for visualization or read point-by-point by a realtime monitoring system to look for anomalies as they occur.

You can find more detailed information about building a high-performance time series database on a NoSQL database in our book, *Time Series Databases: New Ways to Store and Access Data* (*http:// oreil.ly/1ulZnOf*). In that book, we describe general techniques for storing time series data in a NoSQL database like HBase or MapR-DB and give a specific description of how we modified the open source time series database known as Open TSDB to get much higher ingest rates.

CHAPTER 6
Customer Stories

Who is using Hadoop and what are they using it to do?

This chapter is a sampling of some of the ways in which MapR customers are using Hadoop and the NoSQL databases MapR-DB or HBase in real-world settings. Some customers are exploring these new technologies to see how they might want to incorporate them into their organizations. Others have come to Hadoop to find a solution that addresses specific problems they face in dealing with projects at large scale, such as was the case with India's society-changing Aadhaar project. Either way, people are looking for cost-effective and powerful approaches that enable them to reach their goals and, in the case of business enterprises, that help them keep their competitive edge. Hadoop and NoSQL databases are excellent tools to do this.

In this chapter, we provide customer stories so that you can see how some of the prototypical Hadoop use cases we described in Chapter 5 are put into action, often in combination. Many customers employ Hadoop in multiple ways, sometimes starting with a single goal and then expanding how they want to incorporate Hadoop solutions throughout different divisions or projects within their organization. You'll also notice overlap between sectors—some widely different types of organizations share the same underlying technical challenges and so can benefit from the same design patterns in building their solutions. Throughout this chapter, we hope you recognize similarities to your own situation so that you can see what Hadoop might do for you.

Telecoms

Rapid expansion of mobile phone usage worldwide presents telecommunication companies with a variety of challenges in handling enormous amounts of data often arriving at high velocity. These companies must deal with hardware and data issues, as well as direct customer relations. For example, each cell phone tower is constantly communicating with all the mobile phones in its area. Imagine the level of data exchange that is taking place for the billions of phones that exist. People use their phones for all sorts of things: communication with other people through texting, voice, and social media; connection to the Internet; photos; and even financial transactions. Cellular networks are being employed to carry data from machines as well. Usage levels also vary a lot at different times of the day, in different locations, and in response to different events. Imagine the spike in phone usage in an area where there has been a substantial earthquake (assuming the cell towers are still operating).

Telecoms deal with high-velocity and very large-scale data combined with a complicated range of business goals, so their situations are ideal for benefiting from Hadoop. They keep logs of billions of customer transactions and make use of sophisticated machine learning applications such as anomaly detection to monitor and adjust their networks. But in addition to dealing with electronic equipment and acts of nature, telecoms also face all the typical aspects of less-complicated businesses such as marketing, customer relations, and billing. The critical-path reporting that is necessary for billing must handle huge amounts of data, and if this process cannot keep up with the scale of the business, the company will miss out on revenues. This aspect of their business—collecting customer detail call records and analyzing this information as part of the billing cycle—has traditionally been done on electronic data warehouses. The problem is, increasing data volumes are putting a strain on the data warehouses. These data warehouses do not scale as well as needed, and while very good at what they do, they are expensive. We've chosen this story to show you one of the more mainstream but absolutely critical functions for which Hadoop can be useful: data warehouse optimization.

Better use of the data warehouse was the first prototypical use case we discussed in Chapter 5, and telecoms are among many companies that use the MapR distribution for Hadoop to do just that. By collecting customer call records (CDR) on the Hadoop cluster initially, telecoms are able to move the ETL process there as well, thus relieving the data warehouse of this burdensome and expensive task. In some cases, by moving less than 10% of the code associated with the DW billing project to the Hadoop cluster, it's possible to free up a large percentage (commonly as much as 70%) of the load on the DW resource for this process.

Telecommunications reporting and billing is complicated, so it makes sense to continue to use the sophisticated DW resource for the final stages in the process. The enormous initial data volume for CDR data is reduced on the Hadoop platform during the extraction and transformation process. The output is then exported to the data warehouse for the rest of the analysis needed for billing. The data warehouse can more easily handle the much smaller volume of the now-refined data than it could the original call records. Each tool—Hadoop platform and data warehouse—is now being used for what it does best. The result is a system that handles current process loads at a fraction of the original cost and that is positioned to be able to scale as the usage levels grow.

Now comes the part of the story where we see how one Hadoop use case can lead to another. Telecoms have a variety of needs for data exploration and analysis, from machine learning for anomaly detection to analyzing customer relations for better customer satisfaction. Having the initial call record data on the Hadoop cluster provides added value to the DW optimization in that this data becomes available at reasonable cost for these additional uses.

What Customers Want

Figuring out what customers want is a fairly obvious and widespread goal in business, as is the intent of influencing what they want through advertising and product placement. These goals may be obvious, but taking effective action to meet them is not always easy. This task is complicated further by the fact that modern businesses often handle huge numbers of products or offer their services to millions of people globally. The good news is that thanks to the ability to track transactions, to log user behavior on websites, to pay attention to what is being said or photographed via social media, and to track inventory, there's a lot of data to help inform a business about what its potential customers want and how effectively its marketing efforts are in driving those preferences. The quantity and variety of data to do this, however, can be daunting, but not so for companies who have adopted a Hadoop data platform.

A wide range of MapR customers are involved in some aspect of marketing optimization, either for themselves to improve customer awareness and satisfaction with their own products and services or as a marketing service or tool sold to clients to help them with their marketing needs. Some marketing service companies provide information about what is being said regarding a client's offerings based on sentiment analysis applications that make use of social and traditional media. Other companies in this sector optimize advertising placement or auctions or evaluate the effectiveness of the advertising budget of their clients.

Whether a company is concerned with providing marketing optimization as a product/service or with improving their own marketing, there are some commonalities in how they employ Hadoop and NoSQL solutions. Some of these were described in the general use case for marketing optimization in Chapter 5. Collecting data about customer behavior from a wide range of sources and storing this data in a centralized hub is a key architectural pattern for marketing optimization activities. The ability of Hadoop to handle large-scale data in a cost-effective way is a big part of why this is such a widespread use case.

Machine learning models can be used to build recommendations that help make marketing more efficient. One MapR customer used the trick of exploiting search technology to implement and deploy an effective recommender that they built and put into production in just a few months, a very short time-to-value. Companies ranging from online retail to high-tech manufacturers rely on Hadoop to support various aspects of their marketing efforts. It's neither the size of the company nor the product or service they offer that attracts them to Hadoop for this use case, but rather the flexibility and cost-effective scalability of this technology.

DataSong

This rapidly growing company provides retailers with a marketing analytics service. They use MapR for their Hadoop platform to serve as a central data hub. Their CEO, John Wallace, talked about this in an interview with Peter McGowan for a *Data Informed* article.

DataSong's analytics software is used to analyze a wide variety of customers' data to determine the effectiveness of their marketing spend. The analysis even seeks to attribute purchases at the level of the individual shopper. The data includes observations of user behavior on websites via clickstream logs, advertising impression logs, direct mail logs, and more, plus financial transaction data. All this data is loaded onto the Hadoop cluster, processed, and analyzed to provide the client with a weekly report showing the incremental impact of their marketing spend.

Why is Hadoop needed? The more sources of data and the longer the time span loaded on for analysis—say, a year's worth of customer data rather than a month—the more accurate the results will be. Hadoop makes it possible for the customer to have a more accurate report.

The direct advantage for DataSong for using MapR's distribution for Hadoop is the scalability and huge cost savings, including the use of commodity machines instead of expensive big storage hardware. As of June 2014, DataSong was achieving these results with a data hub running on 15 nodes of commodity machines running Linux. This setup handles almost a petabyte of data. The Hadoop platform's low cost of storage, scalability, and ability to handle a wide range of data sources provides DataSong with a lot of flexibility in their choice about the size of retail client they can take on.

Essential to DataSong's growth and success has been the opportunity to focus their efforts and resources on developing their sophisticated analytics applications. In the interview, Wallace attributes this to having "...confidence that with Hadoop and MapR, we had the scalability and cost effectiveness we needed to grow our business."

Reference: "DataSong's Hadoop Bet Paying Off" (*http://data-informed.com/datasongs-hadoop-bet-paying/*) in *Data Informed*, June 2014, by Peter McGowan.

Rubicon Project

Rubicon Project is a trading platform for realtime online ad auctions. Advertisers get to review website visitor data before they bid on advertising in order to improve the chances of their ads being placed with interested parties. The huge volume of data this business must handle was a good reason to turn to Hadoop, and Rubicon selected MapR's distribution.

The auctions Rubicon conducts occur in strict realtime, so they made use of Hadoop ecosystem tool Apache Storm to collect the data and analyze it in connection with bidding and then store it on the Hadoop cluster. This architecture can handle the large data scale while keeping fast response times, as is needed for a realtime auction. Additional data transformation is carried out on the cluster as a preparatory step to ready it for use with traditional applications. This setup is a good fit for Hadoop.

Reference: "Hadoop too slow for real-time analysis applications?" (*http://bit.ly/1KIe48E*) in TechTarget's Search Business Analytics, December 2013, by Ed Burns.

Working with Money

Financial institutions are like many businesses in that they do marketing to prospective clients, track operations, sell and deliver services via a website, and collect and analyze data and process it for billing reports. Hadoop provides a good scalable foundation for many of these goals, as we've discussed. But in addition to these common business activities, banks and other financial firms also handle money—a lot of money—and this responsibility for a huge quantity of funds makes them a natural target for criminals wanting to commit fraud and security attacks. A bank's funds and its customer data are both of sufficient value to tempt thieves, so it's also natural that financial institutions seek effective ways to reduce risk, including fraud detection for credit card transactions (see Figure 6-1) and anomaly detection to thwart security attacks. To meet these needs, financial institutions require serious scalability and reliability. Many use MapR's distribution for Hadoop.

Figure 6-1. Because financial institutions generally must deal with very large-volume and sometimes high-velocity data that needs to be stored reliably and analyzed in a variety of ways, many are among the pioneering users of Hadoop. They also like MapR's ability to use legacy applications along with Hadoop applications.

Risk-reduction activities include some applications to identify known suspicious patterns of behavior in transaction records and website logs. But criminals keep changing how they attempt to steal credit card information or attack a secure site, so financial institutions get help from machine learning models to discover these new patterns of anomalous behavior.

One of the key use cases for financial institutions is *security log analysis*. In fact, this is just a special case of log analysis, but one that is targeted toward looking at log events that might have some security implications. For the mechanics of security log analysis, you can check out the use case information on realtime log analysis described in Chapter 5. Realtime analysis of security is commonly a requirement if you have automated alerts. Whether or not you strictly need realtime analysis, it is not a bad idea to use a streaming architecture for the analysis. There are no significant advantages for a non-realtime architecture versus a micro-batching architecture, and a streaming architecture always has the option for adding realtime alerts.

Another way that financial customers can reduce risk is by having a good disaster-recovery mechanism. One large financial firm using Hadoop wanted to set up a second production data center at a distant site in order to protect a very large amount of critical data. Of course, the first time data is moved to such a secondary center, it is a much bigger project than just updating it. This company set aside two weeks for the initial load of their secondary data center, so they were surprised when the data transfer took less than a day thanks to MapR's mirroring capabilities and a large amount of temporarily provisioned network bandwidth. Subsequent incremental updates to the DR center were extremely fast. (We described MapR-specific mirroring in Chapter 3.)

With a non-MapR Hadoop distribution, the methods for setting up a secondary center for disaster recovery require a bit more effort, but it is an important step to take for critical data. Even without the convenience of MapR mirroring, however, it is still much easier to use Hadoop to set up the secondary cluster than it would be with non-Hadoop systems.

Of course, financial institutions are not the only businesses to focus on risk reduction via security measures, anomaly detection, and disaster-recovery planning. These techniques are useful for those in other sectors as well.

Zions Bank

The difficult detective work of spotting anomalous data against the background noise of normal patterns is an essential effort for Zions Bank, a Utah-based financial company. Zions Bank is a MapR customer that relies on storing over 1.2 petabytes of data on their Hadoop-based platform in order to carry out a wide range of critical functions that include the detection of fraud attempts or other criminal attacks.

They need Hadoop and NoSQL database technology because of the scale of data and range of data sources they must handle. One of their main challenges in getting valuable insights from their large-scale analytics is the problem of spotting the meaningful signals against a high background of noisy data. They have built a specialized security analytics team to work with traditional and nontraditional data sources including transactions and logs. One of their approaches for best practice is to do a lot of testing, especially of new technologies as they become available.

What do they store in their Hadoop-based MapR data platform? They use both structured and unstructured data, which along with affordable scalability is part of why Hadoop and NoSQL are useful to them. Data includes transaction information for online banking and wire transfers, customer databases, and log files from antivirus and firewall systems as well as server logs.

It takes a powerful, flexible, and cost-effective foundation on which to carry out their hunt for the outliers in this morass of data that signal potential fraud or theft.

Reference: "It Takes More Than Technology to Achieve Big Data Success" (*http://bit.ly/14F1Ooj*) in TechTarget's *SearchData Management*, August 2013, by Mark Brunelli.

Solutionary

Solutionary is a leader in delivering managed security services to keep mid-sized organizations and global enterprises safe. Solutionary's patented security analytics technology reduces risk and protects clients' data. To do this, Solutionary runs MapR's distribution for Hadoop on Cisco's Unified Computing System (CUS) to support high-performance analytics.

According to Solutionary president and CTO Mike Hrabik, quoted in a 2014 *Datamation* article by Jeff Vance, it's important to be able to tell "…what happened in the moments leading up a to security event." That's how you identify patterns of suspicious activity. In the past, it was difficult to do this, particularly to do it quickly. Using Hadoop has changed that with a completely new way to deal with large-scale data. Hadoop handles massive amounts of data and can be scaled horizontally as demands grow. Solutionary also requires speed to deal with sophisticated threats. Using Hadoop, Solutionary is able to detect and analyze a suspected security threat across all their clients in milliseconds as compared to as much as 20 minutes with previous solutions.

Solutionary carries out realtime analytics on huge volumes of event and user activity data. Hadoop provides an enormous advantage here: it makes it possible to pull in both structured and unstructured data that can be analyzed on the same infrastructure, something that was not possible with traditional systems. Being able to use a larger range of data formats and larger data volumes while maintaining high performance enables Solutionary to get a much finer-grained view of client traffic, which in turn improves the accuracy of their security analytics.

References: "Is There A Big Data Bubble?" (*http://bit.ly/1Irz29R*) in *Datamation*, February 2014, by Jeff Vance.

"Solutionary Boosts Security with Cisco and MapR Technologies' (*http://bit.ly/1DDFUkA*). Cisco external Customer Case Study, 2013.

Sensor Data, Predictive Maintenance, and a "Time Machine"

Big data is also having a big impact in the real world of machines. In industrial settings, the idea of smart parts is becoming a very important concept. The idea behind smart parts is that complex components such as turbines or generators have a significantly higher value to those who buy them if the components come with a service to monitor and analyze operational data measured inside the component.

The reason for this higher value is simply that the intelligent analysis of these measurements makes it possible to understand what is going on in the system and that, in turn, allows much lower failure rates while also having lower maintenance costs. Consumers are willing to not only pass some of these savings back to the service provider, but they also value lower variability in the operation of the equipment. This trend toward smart is not isolated to vendors who offer this service. A company that retains and analyzes sensor data themselves can get a payoff in big ways.

One payoff is the ability to do *predictive maintenance*. This is a relatively new and attractive concept that is quickly spreading as sensors become more widespread and companies employ scalable solutions such as Hadoop and NoSQL to handle the large data load needed to do this. This topic may be unfamiliar to you, so we describe it here in a bit more detail than familiar use cases. The basic idea is that the companies that operate industrial systems typically have extensive histories on every significant component in their enterprise resource planning systems (ERP) and also have extensive sensor data from the components themselves stored in plant historian software. The ERP histories record where the component was installed and when it was maintained or refurbished. The ERP histories also record information about failures or unscheduled maintenance windows. The sensor data complements the ERP histories by providing detailed information on how the components were actually operated and under what circumstances.

Combining historical information from the ERP with realtime sensor data from the plant historians allows machine learning to be applied to the problem of building models that explain the causal chain of events and conditions that leads to outages and failures. With these models in hand, companies can do predictive maintenance so they can deal with problems before the problems actually manifest as failures. Indeed, maintenance actions can be scheduled intelligently based on knowledge of what is actually happening inside the components in question. Unnecessary and possibly damaging maintenance can be deferred and important maintenance actions can be moved earlier to coincide with scheduled maintenance windows. These simple scheduling adjustments can decrease maintenance costs significantly, but just as importantly, they generally help make things run more smoothly, saving money and avoiding problems in the process.

A Time Machine

The idea of building models to predict maintenance requirements is a powerful one and has very significant operational impacts, but if you use the capabilities of big data systems to store more information, you can do even more. It is common to retain the realtime measurements from industrial systems for no more than a few weeks, and often much less. With Hadoop, the prior limitations on system scalability and storage size become essentially irrelevant, and it becomes very practical to store years of realtime measurement data. These longer histories allow a categorical change in the analysis for predictive maintenance. Essentially what these histories provide is a time machine. They allow us to look back before a problem manifested, *before* damage to a component was found, as suggested by the illustration in Figure 6-2.

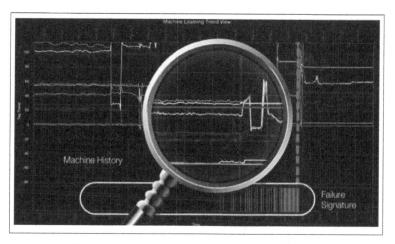

Figure 6-2. Looking for what was happening just before a failure oc-curred provides valuable insight into what might be the cause as well as suggesting an anomalous pattern that might serve as a flag for po-tential problems. (Image courtesy of MTell.)

When we look back before these problems, it is fairly common that these learning systems can see into the *causes* of the problems. In Figure 6-3, we show a conceptual example of this technique. Suppose in this system that wet gas is first cooled to encourage condensation, liquid is removed in a separator, and then dry gas is compressed before sending it down a pipeline.

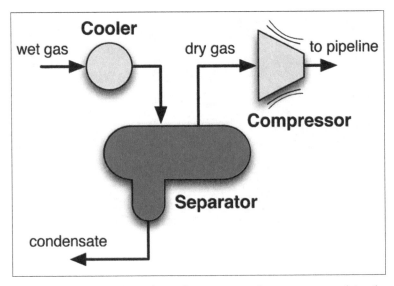

Figure 6-3. In this hypothetical system, a vibration is noted in the bearings of the compressor, leading to substantial maintenance repair action (actually a complete overhaul), but what caused the vibration? We perhaps could have discovered the vibration earlier using anomaly detection, to prevent a catastrophic failure. Even better would be to use enough data and sophisticated analytics to discover that the cause of the pump problems actually was upstream, in the form of degradation in the operation of the cooler.

During operations, vibration is noted to be increasing slowly in the compressor. This is not normal and can result from imbalance in the compressor itself, which if not rectified could lead to catastrophic failure of the compressor bearings, which in very high-speed compressors could cause as much damage as if an explosive had been detonated in the system. Catching the vibration early can help avoid total failure of the system. The problem, however, is that by the time the vibration is detectable, the damage to bearings and compressor blades is already extensive enough that a complete overhaul is probably necessary.

If we keep longer sensor histories, however, and use good machine learning methods, we might be able to discover that the failure (or failures, if we look across a wide array of similar installations) was preceded by degradation of the upstream chiller. Physically speaking, what this does is increase the temperature, and thus volume of the gas exiting the cooler, which in turn increases the gas velocity in the separator. Increased velocity, in turn, causes entrainment of liquid drops into the gas stream as it enters the compressor. It is these drops that cause erosion of the compressor fan and eventual failure. With a good model produced from longer histories, we might fix the cooler early on, which would avoid the later erosion of the pump entirely. Without long sensor histories, the connection between the cooler malfunction and the ultimate failure would likely remain obscure.

This example shows how retrospective analysis with knowledge from the ERP about component failures and previous maintenance actions can do much more than techniques such as anomaly detection on their own. As noted in Figure 6-4, observing the degradations in operation that are the incipient causes of failures can prevent system damage and save enormous amounts of time and money.

Figure 6-4. Early detection of the causes of failure can allow predictive alerts to be issued before real damage is done. (Image courtesy of MTell.)

It is very important to note that this idea of applying predictive analytics to data from multiple databases to understand how things work and how they break employs general techniques that have wider applicability than just in the operation of physical things. These techniques, for instance, are directly applicable to software artifacts or physical things that are largely software driven and that emit diagnostic logs. How software breaks is very different, of course, from the way a ball bearing or turbine blade breaks, and the causal changes that cause these failures are very different as well. Wear is a physical phenomenon while version numbers are a software phenomenon. Physical measurements tend to be continuous values while software often has discrete events embedded in time. The specific algorithms for the machine learning will be somewhat different as well. Nevertheless, the idea of finding hints about causes of failure in historical measurements or events still applies.

The general ideas described here also have some similarities to the approaches taken in security analytics in the financial industry, as mentioned previously in this chapter, with the difference being that security analytics often has much more of a focus on forensics and anomaly detection. This difference in focus comes not only because the data is different, but also because there are (hopefully) fewer security failures to learn from.

MTell

MTell is a MapR partner who provides a product that is an ideal example of how to do predictive maintenance. MTell's equipment monitoring and failure detection software incorporates advanced machine learning to correlate the management, reliability, and process history of equipment against sensor readings from the equipment.

The software that MTell has developed is able to recognize multidimensional and temporal motifs that represent precursors of defects or failures. In addition to recognizing the faults, the MTell software is even able to enter job tickets to schedule critical work when faults are found or predicted with high enough probability, as suggested by Figure 6-3.

The primary customers for MTell's products are companies for which equipment failure would cause serious loss. Not only can these companies benefit from the software, but the potential for loss also means that these companies are likely to keep good records of maintenance. That makes it possible to get training data for the machine learning systems. The primary industries that MTell serves are oil and gas, mining, and pharmaceuticals, all examples of industries with the potential for very high costs for equipment failure.

In addition, MTell's software is able to learn about equipment characteristics and failure modes across an entire industry, subject to company-specific confidentiality requirements. This means that the MTell can help diagnose faults for customers who may have never before seen the problem being diagnosed. This crowdsourcing of reliability information and failure signatures provides substantial advantages over systems that work in isolation.

Manufacturing

Manufacturing is an industry where Hadoop has huge potential in many areas. Such companies engage in a complex business that involves physical inventory, purchase of raw materials, quality assurance in the manufacturing process itself, logistics of delivery, marketing and sales, customer relations, security requirements, and more. After building the product, the sales process can be nearly as complicated as making the product in the first place. As with other sectors, manufacturers often start their Hadoop experience with a data warehouse–optimization project. Consider, for example, the issues faced by manufacturers of electronic equipment, several of whom are MapR customers. They all share the common trait of depending on large data warehouses for important aspects of their business, and Hadoop offers considerable savings.

After initial data warehouse optimization projects, companies have differed somewhat in their follow-on projects. The most common follow-ons include recommendation engines both for products and for textual information, analysis of device telemetry for extended after-purchase QA, and the construction of customer 360 systems that include data for both web-based and in-person interactions.

One surprising common characteristic of these companies is that they have very large websites. For example, one manufacturer's website has more than 10 million pages This is not all that far off from the size of the entire web when Google's search engine was first introduced. Internally, these companies often have millions of pages of documentation as well, some suitable for public use, some for internal purposes. Organizing this content base manually in a comprehensive way is simply infeasible. Organizing automatically by content is also infeasible since there are often secondary, largely social, characteristics that are critical. For instance, the content itself often doesn't provide authoritative cues about which of 40 nearly identical copies of a document is the one most commonly read or cited. Such a mass of information can be understood, however, if you can combine content search with recommendation technology to improve the user experience around this sort of textual information.

These companies also have complex product lines that have a large number of products, each of which is complicated in its own right. This overall complexity produces inherent challenges in the sales process for these companies, and that complexity is exacerbated by the fact that a large customer often has hundreds of contact points that must be managed.

A Hadoop system can help manage this complexity by allowing the creation of a customer 360 use case in which all interactions with customers are recorded and organized. This record can then be used to build models of the sales process and its timing that, in turn, can be used to provide guidance to the sales team. Recommendation technology can be used to build a first cut for these models, but there is a high likelihood that more complex models will be needed to model the complexity of all of the interactions between different sales and marketing contacts with a customer.

Extending Quality Assurance

One very interesting characteristic of large electronic manufacturers is the analysis of telemetry data from the products they have sold. The quantity of data produced and the need for long-term storage to support analytics makes this an excellent use case for Hadoop. Here's the situation. Products that these manufacturers build and sell will often "phone home" with diagnostic information about feature usage, physical wear measurements, and any recent malfunctions. These status updates typically arrive at highly variable rates and are difficult to process well without tools that support complex, semi-structured data. In a sense, these phone-home products extend the period for quality assurance beyond the manufacturing process all the way to the end of the product life. Using telemetry data well can dramatically improve the way that products are designed since real effects of design and process changes can be observed directly. It has even been reported that telemetry data can be used to find or prevent warranty fraud since direct and objective evidence is available about how the equipment is working.

Cisco Systems

Cisco Systems provides a classic story of the evolution of Hadoop use. Today, this huge corporation uses MapR's distribution for Hadoop in many different divisions and projects, including Cisco-IT and Cisco's Global Security Intelligence Operations (SIO), but they started with Hadoop in a simple way. Like many others, Cisco's first Hadoop project was data warehouse offload. Moving some of the processing to Hadoop let them do it with one-tenth the cost of the traditional system. That was just the start.

Seeing Hadoop in the big picture of an organization helps you plan for the future. By making Hadoop part of their comprehensive information plan, Cisco was well positioned to try use cases beyond the original project. It's also important when moving to production to consider how Hadoop fits in with existing operations. You should evaluate your combination of tools for appropriate levels of performance and availability to be able to meet SLAs. Keep in mind that in many situations, Hadoop complements rather than replaces traditional data processing tools but opens the way to using unstructured data and to handling very large datasets at much lower cost than a traditional-only system.

Now Cisco has Hadoop integrated throughout their organization. For example, they have put Hadoop to use with their marketing solutions, working with both online and offline customer settings. Cisco-IT found that in some use cases they could analyze 25% more data in 10% of the time needed with traditional tools, which let them improve the frequency of their reporting.

One of the most important ways in which Cisco uses Hadoop is to support their SIO. For example, this group has ingested 20 terabytes per day of raw data onto a 60-node MapR cluster in Silicon Valley from global data centers. They need to be able to collect up to a million events per second from tens of thousands of sensors. Their security analytics include stream processing for realtime detection, using Hadoop ecosystem tools such as Apache Storm, Apache Spark Streaming, and Truviso. Cisco's engineers also do SQL-on-Hadoop queries on customers' log data and use batch processing to build machine learning models. From a simple first project to integration into widespread architecture, Hadoop is providing Cisco with some excellent scalable solutions.

References: "Seeking Hadoop Best Practices for Production" (*http://bit.ly/1yd4hCy*) in TechTarget, March 2014, by Jack Vaughn.

"A Peek Inside Cisco's Security Machine" (*http://bit.ly/1z8U0s*) in *Datanami*, February 2014, by Alex Woodie.

"How Cisco IT Built Big Data Platform to Transform Data Management" (*http://bit.ly/1u52kCC*), Cisco IT Case Study, August 2013.

CHAPTER 7

What's Next?

We're enthusiastic about Hadoop and NoSQL technologies as powerful and disruptive solutions to address existing and emerging challenges, and it's no secret that we like the capabilities that the MapR
distribution offers. Furthermore, we've based the customer stories we
describe here on what MapR customers are doing with Hadoop, so it's
not surprising if this book feels a bit MapR-centric. The main message
we want to convey, however, is about *the stunning potential of Hadoop
and its associated tools.*

Seeing Hadoop in the real world shows that it has moved beyond being
an interesting experimental technology that shows promise—it is liv-
ing up to that promise. Regardless of which Hadoop distribution you
may use, your computing horizons are wider because of it. Big data
isn't just big volume—it also changes the insights you can gain. Having
a low-cost way to collect, store, and analyze very big datasets and new
data formats has the potential to help you do more accurate analytics
and machine learning. While Hadoop and NoSQL databases are not
the only way to deal with data at this scale, they are an attractive option
whose user base is growing rapidly.

As you read the use cases and tips in this book, you should recognize
basic patterns of how you can use Hadoop to your advantage, both on
its own and as a companion to traditional data warehouses and databases.

Those who are new to Hadoop should find that you have a better understanding of what Hadoop does well. This insight lets you think
about what you'd like to be able to do (what's on your wish list) and
understand whether or not Hadoop is a good match. One of the most

important suggestions is to initially pick one thing you want to do and try it. Another key suggestion is to learn to think differently about data —for example, to move away from the traditional idea of downsampling, analyzing, and discarding data to a new view of saving larger amounts of data from more sources for longer periods of time. In any case, the sooner you start your first project, the sooner you build a Hadoop experience on your big data team.

If you are already an experienced Hadoop user, we hope you will benefit from some of the tips we have provided, such as how to think about data balance when you expand a cluster or find it useful to exploit search technology to quickly build a powerful recommendation engine. The collection of prototypical use cases (Chapter 5) and customer stories (Chapter 6) may also inspire you to think about how you want to expand the ways in which you use Hadoop. Hadoop best practices change quickly, and looking at others' experiences is always valuable.

Looking forward, we think that using Hadoop (any of the options) will get easier, in terms of refinement of the technology itself but also through having a larger pool of Hadoop-experienced talent from which to build your big data teams. As more organizations try out Hadoop, you'll also hear about new ways to put it to work. And we think in the near future there will be a lot more Hadoop applications from which to choose.

We also think there will be changes and improvements in some of the resource-management options for Hadoop systems, as well as new open source and enterprise tools and services for analytics. But as you move forward, don't get distracted by details—keep the goals in sight: to put the scalability and flexibility of Hadoop and NoSQL databases to work as an integral part of your overall organizational plans.

So the best answer to the question, "What's next?," is up to you. How will you use Hadoop in the real world?

Additional Resources

The following open source Apache Foundation projects are the inspiration for the revolution described in this book.

Apache Hadoop (http://hadoop.apache.org)
   A distributed computing system for large-scale data

Apache HBase (http://hbase.apache.org)
   A non-relational NoSQL database that runs on Hadoop

The following projects provide core tools among those described in this book.

Apache Drill (http://drill.apache.org)
   A flexible, ad hoc SQL-on-Hadoop query engine that can use nested data

Apache Hive (https://hive.apache.org)
   A SQL-like query engine, the first to provide this type of approach for Hadoop

Apache Spark (https://spark.apache.org)
   An in-memory query processing tool that includes a realtime processing component

Apache Storm (https://storm.apache.org)
   Realtime stream processing tool

Apache Kafka (http://kafka.apache.org)
   Message-queuing system

Apache Solr (http://lucene.apache.org/solr/)
   Search technology based on Apache Lucene

ElasticSearch (http://www.elasticsearch.org)
   Search technology based on Apache Lucene

The use cases described in this book are based on the Hadoop distribution from MapR Technologies (*https://www.mapr.com*).

For cluster validation, there is a github repository (*https://github.com/MapRPS/cluster-validation*) that contains a variety of preinstallation tests that are used by MapR to verify correct hardware operation. Since these are preinstallation tests, they can be used to validate clusters before installing other Hadoop distributions as well.

Additional Publications

The authors have also written these short books published by O'Reilly that provide additional detail about some of the techniques mentioned in the Hadoop and NoSQL use cases covered in this book.

- Practical Machine Learning: Innovations in Recommendation (*http://oreil.ly/1qt7riC*) (February 2014)
- Practical Machine Learning: A New Look at Anomaly Detection (*http://bit.ly/anomaly_detection*) (June 2014)
- Time Series Databases: New Ways to Store and Access Data (*http://oreil.ly/1ulZnOf*) (October 2014)

About the Authors

Ted Dunning is Chief Applications Architect at MapR Technologies and active in the open source community, being a committer and PMC member of the Apache Mahout, Apache ZooKeeper, and Apache Drill projects, and serving as a mentor for the Storm, Flink, Optiq, and Datafu Apache incubator projects. He has contributed to Mahout clustering, classification, matrix decomposition algorithms, and the new Mahout Math library, and recently designed the t-digest algorithm used in several open source projects.

Ted was the chief architect behind the MusicMatch (now Yahoo Music) and Veoh recommendation systems, built fraud-detection systems for ID Analytics (LifeLock), and has 24 issued patents to date. Ted has a PhD in computing science from University of Sheffield. When he's not doing data science, he plays guitar and mandolin. Ted is on Twitter at *@ted_dunning*.

Ellen Friedman is a solutions consultant and well-known speaker and author, currently writing mainly about big data topics. She is a committer for the Apache Mahout project and a contributor to the Apache Drill project. With a PhD in Biochemistry from Rice University, she has years of experience as a research scientist and has written about a variety of technical topics including molecular biology, nontraditional inheritance, oceanography, and large-scale computing. Ellen is also co-author of a book of magic-themed cartoons, *A Rabbit Under the Hat*. Ellen is on Twitter at *@Ellen_Friedman*.

Colophon

The text font is Adobe Minion Pro; the heading font is Adobe Myriad Condensed; and the code font is Dalton Maag's Ubuntu Mono.

Strata+
Hadoop
—— WORLD ——

Make Data Work
strataconf.com

Presented by O'Reilly and Cloudera,
Strata + Hadoop World is where
cutting-edge data science and new
business fundamentals intersect—
and merge.

- Learn business applications of
  data technologies

- Develop new skills through
  trainings and in-depth tutorials

- Connect with an international
  community of thousands who
  work with data

Lightning Source UK Ltd.
Milton Keynes UK
UKOW06f1537140515

251535UK00013B/82/P

9 781491 922668